NAVIGATING the Winds of CHANGE

NAVIGATING the Winds of CHANGE

LYNN ANDERSON
Foreword by Leith Anderson

HOWARD
PUBLISHING CO.

3117 North 7th Street
West Monroe, Louisiana 71291

Our purpose at Howard Publishing is:

- *Inspiring* holiness in the lives of believers
- *Instilling* hope in the hearts of struggling people everywhere
- *Instructing* believers toward a deeper faith in Jesus Christ

Because he's coming again

Howard Publishing Co., Inc., 3117 North 7th Street, West Monroe, LA 71291-2227

Navigating the Winds of Change

© 1994 by Howard Publishing Co., Inc.
All rights reserved. Published 1994
Second impression 1994
Printed in the United States of America

Cover Design by LinDee Loveland

ISBN# 1-878990-31-4

Scripture quotations not otherwise marked are from the New International Version, © 1973, 1978, 1984 by International Bible Society. Used by permission Zondervan Bible Publishers.

Dedicated to

Andrea, David B., David H., Elaine,
Jeff, Lanny, Lauren, and Lyn

Fellow purveyors of hope
who did the hard work which
enabled *Connects I & II* to connect.

▲

CONTENTS

ILLUSTRATIONS

FOREWORD

Yogi Berra had an insight into the obvious as he said, "When you come to a fork in the road, take it!"

In the 1990s we have come to a fork in the road of history. We do have a choice of *which* road to take into the future, but returning to the past is not an option.

Some yearn for yesterday, hoping and praying that next year will be 1955. But calendars never turn backward.

Personally, I believe that we are at a point of great opportunity and enormous potential. In this respect, the nineties are not unlike the first century. In Galatians 4:4 Paul explains that "when the time had fully come, God sent his Son." The time for Jesus was just right: godly Jews waited for the Messiah, political peace in the Roman empire facilitated the communication of the gospel, and Roman roads and the Greek language joined people together as never before. The time was right, the opportunity was great, and the first-century Christians responded to the challenge to win their generation to Christ and the church.

We want to be like those first-century believers, seizing the opportunity and winning our generation. However, being like them does not mean traveling Roman roads or speaking the Greek language.

If we copy earlier believers in culture and method rather than in spirit and in truth, we compromise true Christianity. To be faithful to Jesus Christ requires that we travel our new roads as they traveled their old roads, that we speak today's language the way they spoke yesterday's language, that we be culturally relevant as they were culturally relevant. In other words, in order to be faithful to the message and person of Jesus Christ and to reach our generation, we must change.

In the pages ahead you will read Lynn Anderson's chart for navigating the winds of change. Anderson unequivocably acknowledges Jesus Christ as the captain of the ship but also recognizes that the winds are blowing in different directions into the twenty-first century than they did into the first century.

—Leith Anderson

PREFACE

Leith Anderson's ground-breaking book *Dying For Change* challenged me to apply sound change principles in the backyard of my own religious heritage. Churches of Christ, like many other Christian fellowships, struggle with change, but in too many situations we are hampered by systemic gridlock and a fixation on the past. Some are held back by fear of the unknown, and some even self-ishly cling to old comfort zones.

But forty years of ministry and observation have deeply convinced me that, as fearful or uncomfortable as some may be, if we are to continue to fill our place in God's global mission, some mid-course correction is overdue. Maybe even, in some cases, we must change or die!

Identifying what must and must not change is our first task. Certain truths are bedrock to the faith. Although this first task is challenging, our second is infinitely more complex: learning how to manage change!

No. I definitely do not pose as an expert on change management! There are no experts; we are learning together. But in my search for answers, I have drawn from several whose expertise I greatly respect: Peter Senge, William Bridges, Charles Siburt, Lyle Schaller, Leith Anderson, George Barna, Randy Lowry, Joe Beam, Chris Argyris, Daryl Conner, Dub Orr, and others.

As I sift, compile, and digest information, my convictions only deepen: we *must* be willing to change. If we are to stop the hemorrhage of young people from our churches; if we are serious about reaching unchurched people; and most importantly, if we are to authentically honor our God—we must be willing to change.

The Christian community is not the only one shaken by the winds of change. Our whole world is reeling from unprecedented degrees of upheaval, and we can learn much from the innovative efforts of the business world to manage change. The principles of this book combine my own thirty-five years of experience, research from other change agents, and gleanings from change management specialists in the business community.

I am convinced that the insights I used to navigate change in my own backyard fit other neighborhoods as well. While some of the illustrations and specific issues in this book relate primarily to my own fellowship, the principles come from a broad base and can be applied across the Christian community.

Several people trudged through the trenches with me as these pages came together. Huge thanks to Carey Garrett, who works professionally in corporate change management. Carey has cotaught seminar classes with me and coauthored much of section five. Special thanks also to Lyn Rose, my assistant who has been the "project supervisor" on this book. Her professional eye and unlimited energy, combined with her irrepressible sense of humor, made even the drudgery fun. Thanks also to Rene Heard who typed several drafts and to Dr. Evertt Huffard, of the Harding Graduate School of Religion, for a thorough critique and helpful input. And, last but not least, to Philis Boultinghouse of Howard Publishing Company. Philis has been more than an excellent, professional editorial technician; she has taken enormous emotional ownership of this book and its prospect for ministry.

My prayer is that God use these pages for his purposes.

▼

"When you see the ark of the covenant of the Lord your God, and the priests, who are Levites, carrying it, you are to move out from your positions and follow it. Then you will know which way to go, **since you have never been this way before.** *But keep a distance of about a thousand yards between you and the ark; do not go near it." Then Joshua told the people, "Consecrate yourselves, for tomorrow the Lord will do amazing things among you."*

Joshua 3:3-5

Like Joshua at the Jordan,
we have never been this
way before.

*F*ACING THE CHILL WINDS OF CHANGE

The opening scene of Larry McMurtry's novel *Streets of Laredo* finds Brookshire, a railroad accountant from Brooklyn, standing in the windy streets of Amarillo, Texas. He has come west bent on hiring Captain Call (a salty old leftover from *Lonesome Dove*) to hunt down a dangerous train robber. Brookshire has never been west before. It's a new frightening world for him. He senses that his life will never be the same again, that he will never get back to Brooklyn.

Brookshire hates the wide-open west, especially he hates the wind, which keeps snatching away his stubby eastern fedora.

The wind lifted his hat right off his head. He was forced to chase it—not the first time he had been forced to chase his hat since arriving in Amarillo. He had taken to ramming his hat down on his head nearly to his eyebrows, but the Texas winds were of a different order than the winds he had been accustomed to in Brooklyn, where he lived. Somehow, time after time, the Texas winds lifted his hat. Before he could even get a hand up to grab it, there it went . . . .

This time the hat rode the wind like a fat bird—it had a twenty-yard lead on its owner before it hit the ground, and when it did hit, it rolled rapidly long the gritty street. Fortunately for Brookshire, a wagon was parked to the south of the station, and the hat eventually lodged against one of the wagon wheels. He strolled over and picked it up, trying to appear nonchalant . . . .

To his surprise, [he] suddenly found that he was feeling a little desperate—he felt that he didn't dare move. The wind had become even more severe, and he had the sickening sense that he, not his hat, was about to blow away. There wasn't a tree in sight that he could see: just endless plain. Unless he could roll up against a wagon wheel, as his hat had, there would be nothing to stop him for days, if he blew away. He knew it was an absurd feeling: grown men, especially heavy men such as himself, didn't just blow away. Yet the feeling persisted, and every time he happened to glance across the street and see nothing—nothing at all except grass and sky—the feeling got worse. . . .

Brookshire began to wish, very much, that he could go home to Brooklyn.[1]

Beginning here McMurtry draws us into a haunting story of change. Captain Call is the last of a dying breed. Familiar ways are vanishing. The winds of change are sweeping away a whole way of life, and the West will never be the same again.

Some time back, an eight-year-old girl stood on a brand-new lumber railway station platform at the little Canadian town of Kincaid, Saskatchewan. Shiny blue steel rails stretched across the prairies to the horizon. Around that little platform circled a colorful collection of buggies and Model T Fords. People were decked out in Sunday-go-to-meetin' clothes. After she was eighty years of age, my mother told me how that day—when as a little girl she first heard the whistle blow and felt the earth tremble as that steam locomotive chugged into the station—she had had a terrified sinking feeling because she knew her world would never be the same again.

The winds of change tugged at her hat and threatened to blow her world away. Mom guessed right! The opening of that railroad signaled several decades of unprecedented change, and not just in her corner of the world. Things have moved so rapidly that, by the time my mother died five years ago, she had witnessed more global change than had occurred in all of history prior to her birth. Of course, the pace of change only accelerates today. And we have less and less idea what will happen next or where it's all going to take us. We are not only driving beyond our headlights—we have run off the maps. Like Joshua at the Jordan, we have never been this way before.

NEW TERRITORY

The winds of change are howling around the church as well. In his book *Dying for Change,* Leith Anderson wrote:

> Everyone is in motion. Each church member is changing while the church is changing while the society is changing. Change is not the choice. How we handle it is.
>
> At the end of the twentieth century, the currents of society are becoming more powerful and the waves of change are crashing closer. It is increasingly difficult for any individual, family, business, organization, church, or community to escape the sweeping changes brought about by drugs, globalization, environmental pollution, political polarization, or economic realignments.
>
> No one is isolated. No one is exempt. Whether for good or ill, whether we like it or not, change is inevitable.[2]

What is stirring this tempest? Countless currents converge, resulting in today's tornado of transition. But three forces have dominated in recent decades. *First,* our world has shifted from an industrial society to an information society. This has created new values—the hottest market commodity today is the creation, transfer, and application of information and services.

People process information in new ways and with lightening speed. The culture keeps few secrets anymore; a home PC terminal can instantaneously access the best data on almost any given subject.

Second, the population demographic presents a whole new paradigm. People live longer and change careers more often. They depend less on corporations for security, on institutions for belonging, and on authorities for answers. As George Barna (church growth researcher and author) says,

> The clock is running and churches who want to stay in the race must adjust to some new realities: Most people

do not believe the Christian Church is relevant in today's world; baby busters are looking for alternatives to traditional religious practices and faiths; fewer and fewer unchurched people express an interest in attending a Christian church in the future; adults are spending less time volunteering at churches.[3]

The pluralization of North America is moving with breathtaking speed as well, sweeping away former moral and cultural assumptions and chopping up the country into a thousand tiny market niches and mission fields.

Third, the restructuring of the economy, both nationally and globally, has made the future uncertain, job security unlikely, and several layers of mid-management nonexistent. Global advertising fills every village with tantalizing images of opulence, while real poverty grows like cancer in every country of the world.

Oh, yes, the winds they are a blowin'. But not all change is bad. Some change is mighty good, and this book picks up on the positive side of change, especially on positive changes in the church.

OLD MAPS

Not long ago, I believed churches could not change. Past literature said they could not. However, I no longer believe this, for I have seen churches change. Current literature chronicles changes in hundreds of organizations, including churches. And today's changes are not merely cosmetic. Basic paradigms are shifting. Profound and speedy changes have catapulted us into "new realities" that make the "old rules" obsolete. If you don't believe me, ask Gorbachev.

Yesterday's "maps" fit times when change came in small units and moved slowly. But today, we have run off the old maps. The fierce winds have blown us into uncharted waters. Anything can happen. So if we are to connect, we must stay ahead of the change curve, continually inventing strategies to manage what is not fully here yet.

However, let me raise a warning flag. Our finest Christian leaders are learning *what* must change; but explosions are erupting in churches all over the country because very few, even of our brightest and best, know *how* to implement or manage desired change. Many sincere attempts backfire, actually heightening fear and hardening resistance, sometimes resulting in congregational upheaval, even in church splits. So it is imperative that we learn to change without trampling on hearts or dividing churches. In fact, at this turbulent point in our history, the most valuable skill we can acquire may well be *effective change management.* With that skill in hand, we may more likely be able to navigate the winds of change without being blown away.

A NEW ART FORM

But the art of change management is a brand-new field, even in the marketplace. Many of today's flourishing corporations assign teams of high-powered personnel specifically to manage organizational change. My own circle of relationships provides a couple of examples: Carey Garrett,[4] a warm and bright Christian woman who works for the largest information management corporation in the country and advises its clients on how to change to improve business performance; Joe Beam, a brother who leads a booming Georgia-based consulting group that helps corporations manage change; and Randy Lowry of Pepperdine University who has not only written an excellent book on conflict management,[5] but conducts seminars and does consulting for church leaders. Of course there are hundreds of other resources and resource people in the field of change management.

Even the literature addressing change has itself become a growth industry. Organizational leaders in corporations, medicine, education, and other fields are tuning in to the research and insights of change management experts like William Bridges, *Managing Transitions;* Peter Senge, *The Fifth Discipline;* Chris Argyris, *Overcoming Organizational Defenses,* and Daryl Connor, *Managing at the Speed of Change,*[6] among others. (See the appendix for resources.)

Two years after Tom Peter's book *In Search of Excellence* described forty-three of the best run companies, fourteen of them were in financial trouble due to failure to respond to change. If business organizations cannot survive the chill and turbulent winds of change without change management skills, can the church expect to flourish without them? Christian leaders, too, must shift paradigms (the ways we see things) if we are to nurture effective churches for the twenty-first century. There is no shelter from the raging hurricane out here on the plains of reality. So hang on to your hat—here we go!

WHY CHANGE?

"For time and the world do not stand still. Change is the law of life. And those who look only to the past or the present are certain to miss the future."

John F. Kennedy[1]

Christian leaders can live with the work, the flak, and the frustration; but we can't live without dreams.

SHATTERED DREAMS

Sometimes the winds of change not only whip your hat off, they can blow your dreams away as well. None of us can live well without dreams, because dreams fuel our vitality. All of my life I have been a compulsive dreamer. Can't keep from it. I think it's because I am part of the human family. Even poems about dreaming enchant us. Remember this song of a dreamer:

> Man is a dreamer ever,
>   He glimpses the hills afar,
> And dreams of the things out yonder,
>   Where all his tomorrows are.
> And back of the sound of the hammer,
>   And back of the hissing steam,

> And back of the wheels that clamor,
> Is ever a daring dream.
> > —Author unknown

BIRTH OF DREAMS

In other words, every big thing we humans have done began between some dreamer's ears. Henry Ford dreamed a sputtering, rattling dream and put the world on wheels. Edison dreamed, and night disappeared. Columbus dreamed, and a new world came into view.

Einstein, while daydreaming on a hill one summer day, imagined riding sunbeams to the far extremities of the universe. Upon finding himself returned, "illogically," to the surface of the sun, he realized that the universe must indeed be curved. This was the beginning of his theory of relativity.[2]

Beethoven stumbled through the woods stone deaf to sounds outside him but with his head full of musical dreams, and he put a song in the heart of humanity. Man is a dreamer—ever!

BROKEN DREAMS

Yet, dark shadows lurk behind our brightest dreams! Another poet hinted broadly that dreams don't always come true.

> We are all of us dreamers of dreams,
> On visions our childhood is fed;
> And the heart of the child is unhaunted, it seems,
> By the ghosts of dreams that are dead.

Only children dream blissfully unaware that some dreams get totally shattered. Life has not yet left them with broken dreams. But sooner or later . . . So the poet moves on:

> From childhood to youth's but a span
> And the years of our life are soon sped;
> But the youth is no longer a youth, but a man,
> When the first of his dreams is dead.

When did you last mourn the death of a dream?

In 1901 a strange sale took place in Washington, D. C. The government auctioned off 100,000 old patents that had never made it to production.[3] The crowd repeatedly roared with laughter at the bizarre contraptions inventors had dreamed up. One was the "automatic bed bug buster": two blocks of wood, with leather hand-holders—one for the right hand, one for the left. Simply place the bug between the blocks and "bust 'im." Didn't sell! Another device was intended to cure snoring. Some inventive hand had simply unraveled a trumpet and attached it to a head harness. The sleeper could strap the mouthpiece to the lips with the big end of the trumpet to the ear. When his amplified snore thundered in his ear, he woke himself. My wife, Carolyn, has been looking for one for me!

An observer of this event said that his laughter died when it dawned on him that he was not listening to 100,000 jokes, but witnessing 100,000 broken dreams. People had invested lifetimes into some of those contraptions. But the inventors had died with broken dreams!

When I drive across the plains and spot one of those lonely, abandoned old houses on the horizon, the collapsing fence corralling a yard of tumbleweed, windows boarded up or gaping empty, I often feel a tug at my heartstrings over the wreckage of someone's broken dreams.

Maybe just now you have looked away from this page and, with a lump in your throat, recalled a broken dream: failed health, a promotion that never came, a shattered romance, a marriage gone sour, a business gone belly-up, a child who went wrong. Most of us will face broken dreams now and again.

After fifty-seven years of living, nearly forty of them in ministry, I know plenty of shattered dreams firsthand. In fact, I think that somewhere along the way, at least for a while, my own Church of Christ fellowship, like many others, lost its dreams.

DYING DREAMS

A brief look at the struggle for growth in Churches of Christ provides insight not only for my fellowship, but for many others as well. In 1865 *The Baltimore American,* one of the leading newspapers in the country in those days, said the Churches of Christ were "the fastest growing denomination in America, beginning only about forty years ago, but numbering now, in the United States alone, over six hundred thousand communicants."

Just think. From 1815-1865, zero to six hundred thousand in only forty years! In 1865, we were a church on the cutting edge of the culture. But not so today!

Somewhere between the 1860s and the 1950s, we began dreaming big *dreams*. As recently as the 1960s we believed the trend was continuing. We were told that from 1865 to 1960 solid growth continued. We said we were still the fastest growing religious group in the country. My college buddies and I dreamed of "taking the world." Our flagship congregation of that day, the Madison Church of Christ in Nashville, was growing explosively! The Herald of Truth (a Church of Christ radio outreach ministry) broadcasts blanketed the globe. Campus ministries flourished. Our foreign missionaries topped six hundred. The media were beginning to notice us. It was the dawning of a new age, and we were part of a movement that would change the planet! Oh, how we dreamed!

Then, somewhere around 1965, as was the trend in many denominations, our growth statistics flattened until 1970, when they dived into a freefall toward oblivion. Many of our nose-counters and number-crunchers predicted that, if those trends continued, Churches of Christ could well disappear early in the twenty-first century. Although figures compiled by Mac Lynn of David Lipscomb University show a net gain of some 3 percent between 1980 and 1990, there is little cause for celebration.[4] First, those statistics included the fast-growing Boston-based group now known as the International Churches of Christ, not really a part of our fellowship, and this skewed the figures considerably. Second, during that period, baby boomers who had left began bringing their babies back to church. But George Barna's research shows they left again in the late 1980s. Thirdly, the population grew by 10 percent,[5] and we have fallen far below those percentages. So at best our growth statistics have only flat-lined. We are scarcely on the road to real recovery.

In some states, we ended the decade smaller by scores of thousands. Throughout the last decade, as I have visited churches, lectureships, and conferences across the continent, almost everywhere I go, tired voices tell me stories of mega efforts yielding meager growth. Our dreams were shattered! Speaking of Churches of Christ, in 1991 Flavil Yeakley (a researcher at Harding University who periodically does a nose count among Churches of Christ) said, "I don't know of any of our older, larger mainline churches that are growing by evangelism."

Yes, some congregations are growing, but very few by reaching unchurched people. Rather, some are "swelling" by consolidating the fallout from failing, dying churches and collecting bodies at the front edge of demographic shifts. As for reaching the unchurched world, most churches are not getting bigger, but smaller. If that were not sad enough, large numbers of our children are leaving the Church of Christ movement or even abandoning the faith altogether. Many other Christian fellowships appear to have suffered similar declines.

Not all is bleak, however. David A. Roozen and C. Kirk Hadaway, in research hot off the press[6] found that some long established churches are now growing—and part of the growth is coming through evangelism. John Ellas, of the Center for Church Growth, has recently discovered good news among Churches of Christ that parallel the findings of Roozen and Hadaway. Some Churches of Christ, fifteen years old and older, are now growing, and a significant part of that growth appears to result from evangelistic activity. However, these churches are (1) updating their evangelistic strategies and (2) viewing evangelism as a process involving the whole congregational system, not merely as an independent "branch" activity of the congregation. This gives me hope. Older churches can change. Established churches can grow. But, at best, we have a long way to go.

A lot of our preachers have lost their dream, too. Some have even thrown in the towel! At a conference in the mid 1980s, I spotted an old friend leaning against the wall, alone, though in a crowded room, staring at the floor, his eyes as vacant as last year's bird's nest. When I asked what was wrong, it seemed as though he took five minutes to drag his eyes up from the floor to mine. Then he spoke for a lot of us, "Lynn, I've lost my dream. What do you do without dreams?" He was only one of hundreds who represent a lost generation of ministers in the Churches of Christ. I find precious few of my mid-fifties peers who are still in the ministry. Dreams died. Many burned out or gave up. But as William Willomon says, "Burnout in ministry is not usually from overwork, but from under-meaning."[7] Christian leaders can live with the work, the flack, and the frustration; but we can't live without dreams.

> He may live on by compact and plan
> When the fine bloom of living is shed,
> But God pity the little that's left of a man
> When the last of his dreams is dead.

EMPTY CHURCHES

A few summers ago, I sat one afternoon on the balcony of a Swiss chalet in the company of several American and European businessmen, eavesdropping on their shop talk. A British fellow piqued my curiosity when he said he decorated the interiors of bars and restaurants in Canada and the United States with the guts of old churches from Europe.

I said, "You're kidding me!"

"Why, no," he boasted, "One bar in Abilene, Texas, has two churches in it!" (I could have told him about some other bars where the churches seemed to have strong representation, but thought the better of it.)

"Really," I marveled, "Have you been doing this for some time?"

"Oh, about ten or twelve years, now."

"Aw c'mon, how many have you done?" (I was thinking maybe one a year.)

"Oh, some months as many as eleven, some less."

Now I'm not quick with numbers, but it didn't take me long to figure out that he had trashed a lot of churches. I was stunned! "Where in the world do you find all those empty churches?"

"Oh, my friend," the young Englishman beamed, "This man John Wesley has been dead for over a century, but he is making me a millionaire. He traveled all over the British Isles. He got off his horse at nearly every crossroads and preached. By the time he was in the saddle again, they were building a chapel in his tracks. They built 'em big and they furnished 'em well all over the UK." He went on: "That was then. But now their great, great-grandchildren, the young folks in Great Britain, aren't interested in that sort of thing anymore. Those old chapels stand empty 'cept for memories. So the descendants build these little chapels on the corner of the property to house memorabilia. To pay upkeep on the chapels, they sell the guts of the old buildings to me, put the shell to the wrecking ball and the land to the realtor."

He rambled on, but my addled thoughts spun off into another world. By bedtime I still couldn't shake the picture of all those empty churches. I lay awake wondering how long before all those buildings from our boom years, back when growth surged and dreams flourished, would gradually grow quiet, stand empty, and then fall to the wrecking crew. My dreams were dying. What do you do, when the last of your dreams is dead? Oh, what *do* you do?

> Let him show a brave face if he can;
> Let him woo fame and fortune instead;
> But there's little to do but to bury a man
> When the last of his dreams is dead.
> —From "To Dream Again"[8]

The winds of change whipped our dreams away. Will they whip us away, too? Will they tumble us out of sight across the plains of the future?

Did you shift in your chair and say, "Lynn, I thought you were a messenger of hope; you sound more like a prophet of gloom and doom?" Well, now we are ready to talk hope. Listen to the winds whisper from the past.

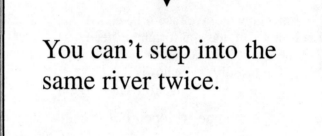

You can't step into the
same river twice.

CHAPTER TWO

WHAT WENT WRONG?

I believe most of our wrist slashing is misguided, and a good deal of the guilt we carry is focused in the wrong place. Self-criticism abounds. Our accusations vary: we are too narrow, too broad, too materialistic, too soft. Some say this generation has lost its first love, that we have sold out our "distinctiveness." Others say that we're too sectarian. Whack! Slash! We berate ourselves almost as if, somehow, we had conspired to make the church go away.

Whoa! Let's think this thing through. While there may be some truth in our self-accusations, I am not convinced that all the good Christians lived in times past. Great people of faith walk in our midst now, at your congregation and mine! Lousy Christians populate the Bible, too. For

starters, check Corinth! Was the nineteenth century or
1950 utopia? No! Something more recent and pervasive
has contributed to declining growth and shattered dreams,
and it has affected nearly all Christian fellowships.

TAUT WINESKINS

The stunted growth of the last few decades cannot be
completely explained by the charges from without and
within that churches are lazy, bad, cold, etc. The thesis of
this book contends that we must also factor in the much
larger issue of cultural change. Jesus' wineskin analogy
(Matt. 9:17) of old, stiff wineskins that couldn't stretch
enough to handle the ferment of new wine fits our day
perfectly. The expanding new wine of today's cultural
changes will eventually burst the traditional, ecclesiastical containers. Supple, expandable wineskins of new
church formats, educational methods, and outreach strategies are needed to accommodate our fermenting culture.

Actually, there was a time when our efforts were very
effective, because those strategies were designed to connect with the culture and were appropriate to the times.
While both the culture and the times have changed,
church strategies, formats, and styles have not. "It is as
if," one pundit observed, "they put my church on autopi-
lot in the fifties and no one has been back to the cockpit
since!"

It wasn't that our message lost its potency. The wine of
the gospel did not run out; rather, the wineskins stopped
stretching. Whatever went wrong, went wrong with many
fellowships, across all denominations. Lyle Schaller,
church growth consultant, reports that "of all local
churches in America which are 25 years old, or older, less

than 5% are growing by evangelism." And of the older churches that are growing, most have "undergone radical systemic and methodological change."[1]

In his book, *Unleashing the Church*,[2] Frank Tillapaugh reminds us that, prior to the American Revolution, churches in this country were mostly cultural branch offices of European denominations, clustered on the eastern seaboard. These churches were led by European trained ministers, who didn't really understand America and did not connect with the new culture. Then, with the Revolution, America headed west and things changed. New churches sprang up all across the frontier, and the church shook its imitation of European churches and shaped an identity uniquely American. Suddenly, churches relatively unheard of moved to the forefront. Baptist plow preachers knew how to communicate with the pioneers. Methodists employed effective "methods." These pioneer church planters designed ways of "doing church" that connected with the culture. The Lord was pleased to bless! Their strategies worked. Church growth exploded. God was doing great things across the West. Often, one of the first large buildings in a new community housed one of those evangelical churches.

STRATEGIES AND TENSION

But that was there and then, and we live here and now! As the winds of time blew across the frontier, settlers drifted toward the great cities. The great-grandchildren of the pioneers graduated from the universities and brought their faith with them to the emerging urban centers. Of course, they wanted the churches to grow in the cities as they had in the country. These Christians followed the old

saying, "dance with the gal who brung ya." In other
words, why scrap the style that brought us here? After all,
these formats had worked back in Farmerville, and "if it
ain't broke, don't fix it." Consequently, rural, frontier
church styles followed other antiques to modern urban
settings. But urban culture was different from rural culture, and the twentieth century is different from the nineteenth.

The pace of change continued to accelerate, the winds
of change rising to hurricane force, with blasts of modernity, mobility, pluralism, and high technology, until those
strategies which served so well in rural nineteenth century
had long since ceased to fit today's cities. They became
less and less effective, until most churches of this style
stopped growing. Today, more than 80 percent of congregations from all denominations are either plateaued or in
decline.

What the plow preachers designed as strategy became
event. Event became *tradition;* tradition became *identity*
and finally *dogma.* To compromise matters, some fellowships slid Bible verses under each practice, so that which
was once only a strategy became "the biblical pattern."
Just one obvious example of a strategy that has lost its effectiveness is revivals: Back in "another life" I used to
hold revivals in rural churches and baptize ten or twenty
people a week. However, few city churches attempt this
strategy today. Most understand that it was designed for a
cultural setting that no longer exists, at least in the cities.

But, not all strategies-turned-dogma die so easily. Old
wineskins resist stretching. Consequently, we are going
through the challenge—new for every generation—of
sorting out what is simply cultural from what is biblical.

And the resulting changes bring *tension*, as we retool to fit our times. But this tension is essential to creating new ministry strategies, organizational formats, and worship styles for effectiveness in our setting.

You may hear someone object, "Now wait a minute. Didn't they get those old strategies and formats from the Bible?" Well, of course, they got their gospel from the Bible. We are not suggesting for one moment that we change anything biblical. If anyone tries to change what is biblical, I, for one, am going to fight. But it is imperative that we change our ways of *expressing* biblical truth and *applying* biblical teaching. We are talking about structuring the church for effectiveness in her mission. We are talking about improving communication and leadership strategies. We are talking about meaningful worship, designed for our place and time, rather than liturgy carried over from nineteenth-century, rural America or eighteenth-century Europe. Did strategies and formats designed by our forefathers effectively express biblical truth in their place and time? Yes! Are those old methods of expresing the message binding on us today? No!

RURAL MINDSETS

We have brought a rural mindset to our urban churches. Some examples you will recognize:

➤ Smaller is better than bigger.

"I feel uncomfortable when I no longer know everyone in the congregation." You do? Just think how nervous you would have been on the day of Pentecost, the birthday of the church, with an instant membership of three thousand. Today's urban boomers have no problem with size. Big surrounds them—big hospitals, big schools, big concerts, big sporting events—big everything. Why would they want little churches? Urban boomers and busters are conditioned to suspect the value of an organization that is so small it can be tracked without a computer!

➤ Sameness is better than variety.

Back in the country, we were nervous when foreigners moved into the community. They were "different." Back then, most people in our churches looked alike. But in today's urban pluralism, sameness is nothing short of segregation. During 1990-91, I worked out of an office in Las Colinas in the Dallas area. Some days, on my way from the parking garage to my seventh floor office, I heard as many as five different languages.

➤ Static is better than change.

"Please keep things as is!" But today, come home from a week's vacation, and you find the corner lot has sprouted a Seven Eleven store! Skylines of our major cities move like the waves of the sea. Things keep changing so rapidly that even blue chip companies like IBM falter when they adjust too slowly.

➤ Classical is more spiritual than contemporary.

Especially in Bibles, music, and prayers. "King James sounds more religious." Not too many urban congregations cling to the King James Bible nowadays, although some still do because they think the language sounds more, um, well, more "reverent." But, our public prayer language is still often King James English—*thees* and *thous* and *thines*—even though we may have long since switched to modern-language translations of Scripture. This quaint tendency to equate classical vocabulary with spirituality would have surprised the apostle Paul. He wrote in the street language of Koine Greek rather than in the more formal, classical Greek.

How about the singing? "I like the grand old hymns. Those new songs are not very spiritual." This sentiment implies that the older it is, the more spiritual it is. Check our hymnals. Few contain more than a half-dozen songs written in this century. As one man said recently, "I want my hymn writers dead. Real dead!" And another, "I'm suspicious of anything written after 1850!" I love those old songs, too. Constellations of sweet memories of long ago and far away cluster around them. I understand the words and the music too, complete with *Ebenezers* and *ebon pinions* because, over a lifetime of Sundays, I have been conditioned to all that, much as one learns a second language. But most modern urbanite boomers, especially the nonchurched, don't understand that kind of music. Both musical idiom and literary style amount to a foreign language for them. Rumor has it that one guest wondered "what kind of fertilizer does it take to raise Ebenezers?" Another questioned whether he would be welcomed spending the night with Ebon Pinion—said he didn't even know where Ebon lives. And one astonished visitor wondered what really happens when an angel's prostrate falls.

Sometimes we have heard people say, "Well, this new stuff is not dignified enough for the church." Interestingly, standard in most evangelical hymnals are old favorites written by Fanny Crosby—"Blessed Assurance," "A Wonderful Savior," "To God Be the Glory," "Praise Him, Praise Him," "Tell Me the Story of

Jesus," "Redeemed, How I Love to Proclaim It!" "I Am Thine, O Lord," "Jesus, Keep Me Near the Cross," "All the Way My Savior Leads Me," and "Rescue the Perishing." But when Fanny wrote those songs a century ago, "respectable" churches wouldn't sing them because they were some of that "contemporary" stuff, lacking liturgical dignity. But let music age a century, and it becomes acceptable. Let it age two or three centuries, and it is classical, sacred music—the heritage of the centuries! Every classical composition was contemporary at one time. But these days, it would hardly be considered normal for a newscast to be in the King James language of the year 1611. And very few radio stations would try to peddle centuries-old, classical, choral music. These are not the heart languages of today's culture.

➣ Peace is better than progress.

Understand, I'm not advocating chaos. But, I do not know of a church in our fellowship today that shows any real signs of vitality that is not also feeling a certain level of growth tension. No, not splits and fights, but the kind of ferment, positive tension, and flux that characterizes growing organisms, especially in our day of dizzying change, bewildering complexity, and fierce competition.

➣ Insiders are more important than outsiders.

Unfortunately, this unspoken, but powerful, assumption is another holdover from closeknit rural communities of the past. Today we may verbalize the opposite. But, when push comes to shove, far more congregational money, time, and effort is expended to accommodate the "already saved" than "to connect with the unchurched."

Yet, Jesus' priorities were clear; "It is not the healthy who need a doctor, but the sick" (Mark 2:17).

PREOCCUPATION WITH THE PAST

What are we saying? Not that former Christians have failed. Quite the opposite! But we are saying that the culture has moved on past them and past many of us. For us to imitate the forms and functions of even very successful churches from former times will doom us to failure. Those forms and functions don't fit the heart language of our current culture. We must reconnect. And this means costly, painful change.

Early Christian leaders in America were far more in touch with the culture of their day than we tend to be with ours. Some preachers helped draft state constitutions, built universities, and designed communications systems. In fact, they were not merely in touch with their culture, they were creating it; their hands held the levers which drove the culture. Thus, the spread of the evangelical Christian movement exploded in those early years.

However, in more recent times, strategies became institutionalized. Today, many congregations hold as sacred the forms and methods which were designed for another place and time. Many churches turned inward, and equated modernity with liberal theology and change with apostasy. Some of us stopped developing, and the culture moved on without us. Consequently, we have difficulty connecting with the people who live here and now.

Of course, without question many churches are hampered on one hand by secularism, liberalism, softness, lack of discipline, and lack of commitment; and on the other hand by narrowness, legalism, sectarianism, exclu-

siveness, and judgmental attitudes. But a much larger im-
pediment to effective outreach of recent decades has been
our preoccupation with the past, our feeling that oldness
equals faithfulness, that past is piety, and that a commitment to the status quo preserves spiritual security. Thus,
in attempting to duplicate church patterns from the nineteenth century—or the first century—we are not effectively projecting the biblical Christ into twentieth-century
experience. Encumbered by a rural mindset, protective of
past ways, we have fallen behind, drifted out of touch,
hardened our categories, and lost our way. Yes! The time
has come when we simply must reconnect.

We must face the future. And by God's grace, we will!
Hope is on the rise. We must boldly navigate the winds of
change. And I believe we are! We are dreaming again. We
are relearning how to connect with the culture. Not only
are chill winds of change blowing, but mighty winds of
renewal are also sweeping the land. I am excited about the
future.

We must dance lightly on
the balls of our feet in
order to connect with an
ever-changing culture.

WHY CHANGE?

This book is about change, but not because I have some sort of fixation on change. It runs much deeper than that. For openers, my grown kids have been working on my heart. They are involved in kingdom business wherever they live. For that I am grateful. But they have repeatedly said, "Mom and Dad, there are two things we want more than anything else in this world. One, we want to worship God with freedom and authenticity, in our own heart language. And two, we want to bring lost people to Jesus and into a church environment that makes sense to them." Now, although our children have visited scores of churches, and been part of not a few, they are implying,

"Frankly, folks, in a lot of the churches we've seen, those things are not happening."

I'm afraid my kids are right. But to be honest, I'm not all that comfortable with change myself. When the alarm went off this morning, I didn't want to move. I like things stable, predictable, comfortable. William Bridges says, "Those who say they do like change, mean that they like to change other people."[1] But my natural inertia and discomfort have been bulldozed aside by some compelling forces. I have become passionately interested in change that can accomplish the two things my kids say are important to them: authentic and free worship of God in our own heart language and a church situation that makes sense to the people we are trying to lead to Christ. However, I am not passionate about this because my children are, but because I believe authentic worship and effective outreach are at the center or God's agenda! Consider with me eight reasons I believe we *must* change.

➤ Many congregations must change or die.

In the decade ahead, unless we change our way of "doing church" we will only become more obsolete and less effective. Refusal to change outmoded methods inhibits growth and ultimately could put many churches out of business. We have been on a double-decade collision course with oblivion. Many congregations are long since gone!

It is not sheer alarmism to suggest that we must change to "stay in business."

➤ **Most churches must change to keep our new generation from continuing to leave.**

In recent years, our young people have been rapidly exiting our churches. While living in Abilene, I visited the Dallas/Fort Worth Metroplex several times each year to speak at various events. Every time I came, I would be taken to quiet corners or out to coffee by former students of Christian universities who were struggling for spiritual survival. Several hundred in Dallas alone, who were once very much involved in the Church of Christ have gone to other fellowships. Hundreds of others worship nowhere. Still other hundreds have given up and headed back into the world. They were dying in too many of our churches. Many found no clear resources for their age and their issues. Few found small groups to nurture them or personal, hands-on shepherding. Worship and church calendars were not designed for their needs. This scene is duplicated in too many cities across the country.

Changes are overdue, particularly in worship style. We must make worship more authentic by speaking and singing in the heart language of our times. We have no trouble understanding why missionaries to Moscow must speak Russian. Yet, antiquated, rural styles of worship and religious communication are as foreign to young people of urban, contemporary America as is English spoken in Russia. Is it any wonder that young people are leaving those kinds of churches in droves—going either to a community church or to some other kind of church that makes sense to them, or giving up and heading back into the world?

Maybe worse yet, many *do* stay and merely go through the motions, but they develop no vital connection be-

tween their beliefs and the practical and relational realities of their daily lives. For many, the church, if it has
meaning at all, is merely the context of their cultural, social, and familial fabric—not a place of genuine worship,
whole-life development, and living relationship with the
living God. If we do not change that, young people will
continue leaving staid churches for churches where the
language of worship and the formats of ministry make
sense to them.

But let's switch our attention to some more positive
reasons for change.

➤ We must change to keep pace with changing needs and opportunities.

Not only do needs and opportunities change with time,
they also change with locale. They are different in
Chicago than in Dallas than in Los Angeles than in
Atlanta. And they are different for Dallas in 1994 than for
Dallas in 1952. So we must dance lightly on the balls of
our feet and constantly change strategies and formats in
order to connect with an ever-changing culture. New
times bring new tools and demand new tactics. Mega-
churches, for example, are enabled by a tool called the
freeway. A few years ago, mega-churches were virtually
impossible, because no transportation arteries existed that
were capable of assembling large numbers of people so
quickly. Other new tools include CNN, computers, video
cassettes, mini-cams, fax machines, fiber optics, and a
thousand more which create new consumer expectations
and new performance capabilities. These phenomena
have enormous implications for the church. If we totally
ignore the reality of massive, swift, and irresistible cul-

tural change going on around us and make no effort to re-tool in order to connect with our culture, we will only fall farther and farther behind.

➤ We must change in order to grow.

Of course, not all change is good, nor does change automatically produce growth. But a strange elliptical truth surrounds change and growth. Growth and change are Siamese twins. In order to grow, we must change. Then growth in turn demands more change. If you don't believe me, ask Moses. When the task of leadership became too large for him to keep in his head and manage personally, Moses had to change. Jethro helped Moses restructure his whole organization and management style because growth had produced change. He had to break things down into smaller units. It works that way in growing churches too. As one man said, "To get bigger, we've got to get smaller." As churches grow, emphasis must be given to relationships in small groups. Large groups create an impersonal atmosphere and thus stall growth. The impersonal nature of our urban culture leaves people hungry for relationships and a place to belong.

With growth, larger meeting places must be provided. Organization must be streamlined. Times, locations, schedules, and calendars must change. Financial needs change. Leadership demands new styles and roles. Expectations change. For example, a preacher might be able to visit all the sick in the hospital when the congregation is two or three hundred, but not when membership reaches one thousand. Especially in urban settings, visitation by the minister becomes impossible. Also, when a church is two hundred, the members can all know each other. At one thousand they will not all know each other, although they may still know two hundred. Growth changes these and a thousand other things. Change is a consequence of growth. And growth is a consequence of the right kinds of changes managed in the right way.

> **We must change in order to effectively reach unchurched, lost people.**

Let's face it: we are not leading many unchurched people to Christ. And of the few truly nonchurched people who are baptized, not many get assimilated into the body and nurtured into spiritual maturity! Since 1980, cites George Barna,

> There has been no growth in the proportion of the adult population that can be classified as born again Christians. The proportion of born again Christians has remained constant (32%) despite the fact that churches and para-church organizations have spent several billion dollars on evangelism. . . . Despite widespread opportunities for exposure to the Gospel, there has been no discernible growth in the size of the Christian Body.[2]

If the cultural language of our assemblies is somewhat befuddling and uncomfortable to churched young people, imagine how little sense it makes to nonchurched visitors! Music, vocabulary, design, and style must be updated so that we connect with the minds and hearts of today's seekers.

However, far more than assemblies must change if we are to connect with nonchurched people and assimilate them into the body of Christ and nurture them on to maturity. Our very structures need to be constantly reevaluated and adjusted, revamped or replaced as the need may be. Such things as assembly times, class times, curricula, and educational styles must be made user friendly to nonchurched people and new converts.

In our ever changing culture, church programs and formats enjoy very short shelf-lives. Therefore, like Paul, we must constantly "become all things to all men . . . [to] save some" (1 Cor. 9:22). That is, we must be willing and able not only to change, but to keep our fingers on the pulse of the culture. We must constantly update formats, schedules, strategies, and methods, moving with the ebb and flow of the people we are trying to reach—the people who matter so much to God! Oh, yes, if we are going to make disciples and "teach them to observe all Jesus commanded," things have got to change significantly. Something has got to give!

➢ We must change in order to worship God more authentically—in the heart language of our day.

As important as teaching, evangelism, service, and social action are, they are not the central purpose of the church. The central focus of the church is *worship.* Actually, the sequence *begins* with worship: (1) worship takes us to God; (2) worship results in life change; (3) life changes result in service; (4) service underwrites the credibility of evangelism. Fortunately, we are in an upsurge of renewal in worship these days. The breathing of life back into a declining church begins with the breathing of life back into worship. But the spirits of worshipers do not get connected with God through language they do not understand or through music that is alien to their heart language.

Antiquated musical idioms, classical music, religious
jargon, and King James English do not engage the hearts
of many of our young people, and certainly not of those
who have been reared outside the church. Some who have
been reared in the church have been conditioned by a lifetime of church-going to understand the language of our
religious heritage. But, although they may well understand the words, sounds, and symbols at church, these
may be incongruent with the rest of their lives. Many feel
that to connect with church they must enter a time warp
or step back into a former era, maybe even into another
reality. Formal and nonparticipatory assemblies that are
primarily cerebral and passive may have fit a bygone culture. But today, the whole person longs to enter into worship—to express, to experience, to actively participate in
the exaltion of God, using today's language, idioms, and
structures.

Make no mistake about it: if worship is to be authentic
and freely expressed in the heart language of today's people, it must undergo mega-change.

➤ We must change in order to mature Christians and equip them for ministry.

Few congregations have any kind of user-friendly track
designed to assimilate and mature and equip new converts—to guide them step by step, from the street, through
the heart of the church, to spiritual maturity and active
ministry. We must revamp educational and assimilation
processes to help busy, lonely Christians in a busy, lonely
world develop the skills to flourish spiritually in their hos-
tile, secular environment. We must learn how to lead people intentionally along a user-friendly path of life

development from the street where they live, through the church, to the heart of God, and then equip each one for the specific ministry that fits his or her gifts and passion. This calls for far more than cosmetic changes in the basic infrastructure of most congregations.

➤ **We must change—constantly upgrade and refine— to maintain excellence, thus glorifying God.**

God deserves our very best. We must offer our very best to him and, in his name, to the people we are attempting to serve and reach. Besides, quite pragmatically, in our excellence-oriented society, the church and the Christian message will not be taken very seriously unless the way we do things shows seriousness by its quality and excellence. In middle-class North American settings, messy buildings, sloppy programs, haphazard educational offerings, outdated methods, irrelevant issues, bad music—all of these send the signal to the nonchurched person: "These church people are out of touch with current reality, and they really don't think what they are doing is very important; so why should I waste my time there?" Excellence in other settings may be measured in terms of acceptance of people different from ourselves, or in genuine active service to the community, or in such things as the quality and consistency of evangelistic outreach.

Yes, it is difficult, challenging, and ever so costly to maintain excellence in an ever changing environment. But to echo the words of King David, "I will not sacrifice to the Lord my God burnt offerings that cost me nothing" (2 Sam. 24:24).

Change is costly, yes. But God and the people who
matter to him are worth it. The problem is that many of us
have already advanced on change many times, only to retreat with egg on our faces. It leaves us wondering: Is it
really possible for a church to change?

IS CHANGE POSSIBLE?

The God who never changes, constantly changes everything.

> "Everything about being a
> Christian means change."

*Y*OU *CAN* TEACH AN OLD DOG NEW TRICKS

Be careful what you say. Words can come back to haunt you, especially if they get into print. I know first-hand.

My friend's voice sounded weary over the phone. "Lynn, you were right. It's hopeless. Old churches can't change. I'm tired of beating my head against brick walls. So what do I do? I don't think I have what it takes to plant a new church. Besides, my wife couldn't handle the financial uncertainty of church planting. I give up. Over and out. Out of the ministry. Maybe out of the church."

"Wait a minute," I objected, "That's not what I had in mind." Although I had meant to traffic in hope, inadvertently I had contributed to my friend's despair.

He had read an interview I had done some months earlier with *Image Magazine*, in which I had said, "Churches, like people, have stories, and once a church's story is established (and by the time it is twenty-five years old, it is very definitely established), you can't change it a great deal. You can clean up some habits here, change some cosmetics there, but the basic nature of that church will remain unchanged."[1]

What can I say? I was wrong. I have changed my mind. I'm still passionately convinced that we *must* plant new congregations that will be more culturally appropriate to our times if we are to effectively reach lost people in our culture, but I am not about to give up on all old churches. Several realizations have revived my hope that some old churches can change enough to reconnect with our times.

CHANGE *IS* POSSIBLE

➤ The map has changed.

True, the literature of the past couple of decades says that churches can't change. And church growth researcher Lyle Schaller told a gathering of preachers that since declining churches can't likely change, we must "plant or perish." I accepted that assessment—concurring that you can't teach an old dog new tricks. Hence the *Image* interview stating that "churches can't change."

But, my conclusions were built on what has happened in the past, not what can happen in the future. My map was obsolete. Rapid change has run us off the old map.

"Poor Henry Ford has lost his mind. Says he is going to manufacture buggies that will need no horses. Gimme a break!"

"Come on now, Mr. Wright. Fly? It can't be done. Look at history."

"No, no, Mr. Galileo. That is *not* how the universe works. Ask anyone from the beginning of time until now."

These comments have two common denominators: first, they were dead wrong; and second, they were founded on old systems—old paradigms that did not allow for the astounding changes that were already in motion. As paradigms shifted, expectations changed.

When I said that churches couldn't change I was wrong too, and for the same reason. The past taught, "Don't try to change a church. It won't work." But the underlying paradigms of our culture are shifting so swiftly and profoundly that what experience has taught us does not necessarily hold true for the future. As we have run off the maps of scientific and technological folklore, so also we have run off the maps of organizational culture and organizational psychology. Reality has shifted.

For example, in his book *Future Perfect,* Stanley M. Davis asserts, "In the industrial economy, our models helped us to manage aftermath, the consequences of events that had already happened. In this new economy however, we must learn to manage the beforemath; that is, the consequences of events that have not yet occurred."[2]

Davis's thesis is that much current management theory was designed to operate organizational structures that were obsolete by the time the theory had been published.

The old rules are off. Paradigms concerning organizational cultures have shifted. We are sailing in uncharted
waters and encountering what Peter Drucker calls "new
realities."[3]

Again, the profound cultural paradigm shifts which
alter the ground rules of change in the marketplace obviously impact churches as well. We can no longer assume
that "as things have been so shall they always be."

So, at least for now, I have significantly modified my
point of view. I have come to believe that, in spite of the
testimony of the past, not only can churches change, but
many have changed, and others must change or die.

➤ People change.

Like you, I have actually seen some individuals
change—and radically. Once I was fired then rehired
three days later. A decade later, one of the elders who had
aggressively favored my firing wrote a long letter of pro-
fuse apology to Carolyn and me. Then, point by point, he
explained significant ways in which his thinking after the
age of seventy had changed.

Another example: A visible change agent in our fellowship is Rubel Shelly. I fondly regard him as a dear
friend and colleague. And I stand in awe of his giant intellect and God-impassioned heart, which are nudging our
movement back on track with the text and helping us better connect with our culture.

But Rubel has definitely changed! Years back he used
to "write up" some of us, even challenging us to debates.
These days he frequently blesses ideas he once blasted
(and gets blasted by folks he once blessed!). His courage
and integrity have kept him growing. I'd hardly call my

beloved friend Rubel an old dog, but without question he has learned some new tricks. Strong people can change. Growing people will change.

➤ Congregations change.

We have also seen whole congregations change. Leith Anderson's watershed book, *Dying for Change,* case-studied an old and declining city congregation that changed enough to become a flourishing church again.[4] The successful renewal of Leith's church gave a lot of us hope that things can change where we are too.

Several visible congregations in the Churches of Christ have also changed dramatically. The Richland Hills Church of Christ in the Dallas/Fort Worth Metroplex was once an ordinary mainline congregation. But about fifteen years ago, after thorough self-examination, her leaders deliberately retooled their ways of doing things in order to connect more effectively with their community. Richland Hills looks vastly different today and has grown to over three thousand.

The Highland Church of Christ in Abilene, Texas, is a much different congregation than it was twenty, even five, years ago. In the late 1970s her elders made a conscious decision to be more like shepherds and less like a board of directors. Then, at fifty-plus years of age, she experienced a significant shift in structure and method, even in worship assembly style. Today, Highland is enjoying yet another period of revival and is connecting with the culture in Abilene, Texas, more effectively than ever.

Some three years ago I was called to be the pulpit minister of the Preston Road Church of Christ in Dallas. Yet some fifteen years earlier, I was occasionally "branded" in the Preston Road bulletin as an example of apostasy. Now, I am no less progressive in my thinking than I was fifteen to twenty years ago. So what happened? The Preston Road congregation has changed—profoundly. That is what has happened. Old dogs *do* learn new tricks.

➤ Whole fellowships change.

Not only do individuals and congregations change, but whole denominations change. The Church of Christ fellowship is definitely changing. The speakers headlining our lectureships and workshops represent a breed different from those of fifteen to twenty years ago.

Our views have changed, too. For example, the personal indwelling of the Holy Spirit in the hearts and bodies of Christians is generally assumed these days. But this was "new and dangerous" teaching just two decades ago in our Church of Christ fellowship. At that time, the common view was that the indwelling of the Holy Spirit was limited to the indwelling of the Word (inspired by the Holy Spirit) in the hearts and minds of Christians. In fact, the terms "Holy Scriptures" and "Holy Spirit" were often used interchangeably. Fortunately, men like Jimmy Allen and Carl Spain stepped forward and helped us rethink the work of the Spirit.

We even look different! Some readers may have been told about times in Churches of Christ when kitchens in the church building, family life centers, gymnasiums, youth ministers, special singing groups, etc. were suspect in many of our churches and flatly verboten in others. Not so now!

Also, two decades ago cutting-edge Church of Christ journals like *Image, Leaven,* and *Wineskins* would have been filed in the dangerous fringe category for most of our congregations, but today they appeal to a broad cross section of our fellowship. And the yellow journals that terrorized our fellowship two decades ago have painted themselves into a corner of low circulation and even lower credibility.

Preaching is changing. Topical preaching, which was once standard fare in our pulpits, is giving way to textual, expository preaching in user-friendly language.

Fifteen to twenty years ago some of us were blacklisted from the major forums in our fellowship and had numerous revivals canceled. That lasted for nearly a decade. Yet, nowadays we cannot begin to accept all our invitations. We have not become more traditional. It is the fellowship that has changed. Hang in there, my ministry friends! Your "labor is not in vain"! Things eventually do change!

➤ It is biblical to expect change.

The gospel invites change so radical it is called "new birth" (John 3:5 ff) and results in "new creatures" (2 Cor. 5:17) who then keep on "changing with ever-increasing glory" (2 Cor. 3:18).

As Carey Garrett, change management consultant for EDS Management Consulting Services in Plano, Texas, and coauthor of some chapters of this book, reflects, "everything about being a Christian means change. It means dying to the world in a rebirth that is in itself a major change and life transition. Thus, being a Christian prepares us powerfully for dealing with the changes life presents."

As Paul moved from culture to culture, he shifted strategies. He expected the church on Crete to change and even said the older people should *lead* the charge (Titus 2:1-5). Frankly, I am troubled when I hear comments that older people are hard-liners and cannot change. In fact, I was brooding on this after I spoke in Lubbock, Texas, at Impact, an annual gathering of retired people from Churches of Christ. What a joy these seniors were! These are definitely not hard and rigid people. They are mostly lovers, not fighters. They owned me like a long lost son, and no group could possibly have been warmer or more affirming. Besides, they have had to do a lot of changing merely to survive in this quicksilver world.

Change is a major interest of the New Testament. Look again at Acts 15 and Galatians and the late chapters of Romans. And in Revelation, the seven churches of Asia were warned to change or have their wicks snuffed.

In Scripture, change is not protrayed as merely *possible;* it is *expected!* In our experience, change is a fact, not an option.

No, we had better not change biblical values or teachings. But our methods, strategies, formats, and style will need constant updating. As the late Ira North (once minister of the widely known Madison Church of Christ in Nashville, Tennessee) said, "With the gospel, the Madison church is as conservative as corn pone. When it comes to method, we are as modern as a spaceship." However, change must be managed carefully, responsibly, patiently, skillfully, and biblically.

THE PLANTING CHALLENGE

Change agency is a delicate and difficult challenge whether you are a church renewalist or a church planter. Both are valid and legitimate callings. But both planting and renewal take a lot of hard work over a long period of time. At a Leadership Network conference in Colorado Springs, a group of pacesetting ministers of large evangelical churches took an informal poll. Most of these ministers had some experience in both the revitalization of existing congregations and the planting of new ones. Each wrote down his guesstimate of the energy required to move an existing church from zero to X, as compared to the energy cost of planting a new church and growing it from zero to X. The average ratio was eleven to one! That is, experience told these men that it takes more than ten times as much energy to bring a plateaued old church to a given level of growth as to plant a new congregation and bring it to a similar level of growth. That poll, of course, was hardly scientific. But most of us who have attempted both planting and renewal would resonate with it.

Three decades ago, many Bible majors in Church of Christ colleges wanted to plant churches, and many congregations were planning daughter churches. Nowadays, existing congregations often see new church plants as a threat and church planters as somehow potentially subversive. So, graduating Bible majors tend to seek the security of established pulpits rather than take the risk of planting new churches.

Yet, others in the evangelical world are experiencing incredible growth rates through new plants. For example, the Southern Baptists have started more than two hundred congregations in just one state during the past year alone!

BEND, BUT DON'T BREAK

However, in spite of the fact that renewal of existing churches may be much slower and more challenging than church planting, renewal is not only a valid, but an important ministry. Frankly, it is the central focus of my own energy these days. But as we attempt to view the situation realistically, we must accept that not all congregations can change; maybe not all should.

Based on my observation of current trends, I think we can make educated guesses as to the likelihood of change in existing churches.

➤ **Some congregations will not be able to change at all.**

Some congregations—even though they are dwindling and will soon die—will cling to the status quo.

➤ **Some congregations, although unable to change, may not die.**

At least, they won't die in the near future. But if they survive, it will likely be only as a sport or an art form. At one time, international travel required sailing, and raising cattle required riding and roping. Today, however, sailboating regattas and rodeos exist only as sport for those who like that sort of thing. In the sixteenth century, some forms of music were popular worldwide that today are merely quaint art forms preserved by a few special-interest musicians.

Just so, some surviving churches will serve only a limited circle. Although at one time their strategies and formats were culturally appropriate and produced explosive growth, today, those outdated forms appeal primarily to a small nostalgic segment who may appreciate that sort of thing. But if we are to significantly impact our world, new times demand new formats.

➤ Some congregations will appear to grow, but in reality will be "swelling."

A number of congregations in key urban areas will experience only the illusion of growth, as rural people move to the city or as city people migrate from dying urban churches to newer (but still traditional) suburban churches. But this will merely consolidate our failures. These "swelling" churches may look successful in the short term but will probably make no significant inroads to the unchurched population. And in the long run, when dying rural communities and failing urban churches can no longer supply believing warm bodies to these newer suburban churches, many suburban churches, which now appear to be growing, will face major crisis, if not total demise.

➤ Some congregations will be able to change some.

Some congregations will be able to change enough to grow slowly and reach at least some pockets of unchurched people, but many of these churches will experience tension concerning what and how fast to change. For many of these congregations, change may not necessarily mean becoming "contemporary," but simply refining the quality, vibrance, and meaningfulness of traditional worship and relationships.

➤ **More and more congregations will change enough
to grow significantly by reaching unchurched peoples.**

This is the really good news! Remember, 5 percent of
congregations twenty-five years old or older are growing
by evangelism because they have changed. The fact that
5 percent have changed and adjusted enough to grow
proves that old churches can change. A number of us
dreamers believe that soon the 5 percent can expand upward to 10, 15 or 30 percent and hopefully, even much
more. This may be especially true

- as God renews our focus on word, worship, and
  witness.
- as God refines our understanding of the message.
- as we learn more about the culture and become
  sensitized to it.
- as our leadership skills expand.
- as we gain skills in the art of change.

We are pioneering a new frontier that is of yet mostly
unexplored. But what others are discovering about the organizational culture of the marketplace matches the dynamics of change we are experiencing in the church. So,
while change strategy in our times is yet a budding science, already the explosion of helpful discovery in this
field convinces me that intentional changes in the organizational culture of churches—changes considered impossible only a decade ago—will soon be commonplace.

Most importantly of all, we trust in the God of changes
—a God who made Ezekiel's dry bones dance! The God
who himself never changes constantly keeps changing
everything. He is changing nearly every religious body.
He is changing the fellowship of which I am a part. We

are becoming more pluralistic and less rigid—a kinder, gentler people. We are beginning to celebrate the many different church styles and strategies being created in honest attempts to reach unchurched people with the one and only and never changing gospel of the Lord Jesus Christ. We are learning that each believer has his or her own unique gifts and calling and that all have their place—renewalists, planters, and traditionalists.

So, in spite of the exciting new church plantings, some on the drawing board and others already on the ground, renewal of old churches is still a valid ministry. Don't lose heart, my brothers and sisters. Every major metropolitan area on the continent needs at least one church that can be a model of healthy change: an old church that learns how to connect with new times and to reach people not now being reached from our traditional churches.

Of course, renewal alone is too slow, too limited, and too late to reach all of our ever changing, rapidly growing, and pluralistic continent. Thus, in addition to renewing old churches, we must begin new churches that look different. In fact, at this very hour, a number or these new churches are already launched. Let us all pray for these pioneers and encourage them as they sail off into uncharted waters. However, renewal is still a major theme of God's global strategy.

Now is not the time to throw in the towel. You *can* teach old dogs new tricks. Believe me—I've seen it. Great days lie ahead. Read on.

WHAT MUST NEVER CHANGE

"Jesus Christ is the same yesterday and today and forever."
Hebrews 13:8

"Don't confuse babies with bath water!"

Why not design worship that *pleases God?*

ℱORM FOLLOWS FUNCTION:
Theological Foundations

A major disclaimer and warning: If your engine is bad, it won't help much to give your car new tires and a paint job. Change within the church must go much deeper than tinkering with formats, strategies, styles, and programs. In fact, if you want your church to have more spiritual horsepower, fiddling with externals is the wrong place to start. Change must first be approached theologically. Good theology may call for strategic changes in format and method. But even the slickest tool kit of change strategies and theories, if not preceded by sound theological reorientation, should be labeled "extremely dangerous."

63

"THE TRUTH WILL SET YOU FREE"

There is no more cruel taskmaster than bad theology. But good theology can free people from the fear of change. For example:

> if our security rests in the church,
>
> if we see restoration as reproducing carbon copies of "the" first-century blueprint,
>
> if we feel that we have already completed the restoration task,
>
> if we believe our salvation rests on the accuracy with which we duplicate that blueprint;
>
> then we will see no reason for change. In fact, we will actually fear change, lest it put our souls at risk.

Tragically, in some quarters, the views just outlined are bedrock assumptions. This is one reason good theology must precede strategy.

But, on the other hand,

> if we see Jesus himself as the blueprint for all people in all times,
>
> if we view the restoration as restoring men and women to Christ,
>
> if this ongoing mission is compelled by gratitude to our gracious God;
>
> then, rather than fearing change, we will eagerly pursue any change that glorifies him more authentically and more effectively restores people to him. And we will more clearly understand what must and must not be changed.

Clinging to a past church model or method, however wonderful it may have been in its heyday, is not a sign of faithfulness. Rather, faithfulness to Jesus' mission requires us to explore every possible model for "doing church" and to continually come up with new methods to restore people to God.

APPROACH CHANGE THEOLOGICALLY

Many of today's suggested changes center on worship in the assembly. Too many of these change attempts begin with the *forms* of worship without addressing the *function*. But before we tinker with change in worship, we must know what we are trying to do when we worship. We dare not tamper with forms, without understanding theological function, lest the altered forms skew the God-intended function of worship.

For example, we may attempt to adjust the forms of worship to the desires of the congregation. This gets tricky because most congregations have at least three main constituencies: some progressives, some traditionalists, and some who are middle-of-the-road. Attempts to design worship for any one of these leaves two-thirds of the church unhappy every Sunday.

Or we may attempt to adjust the forms to connect with the unchurched. This raises two questions: (1) Which unchurched people? Most urban communities are a mixed bag. But even if worship targets a specific segment of the community, question two raises its head: (2) How can assemblies connect with contemporary secular culture and traditional church culture at the same time?

Why not try this novel approach? Rather than beginning with the church constituencies or the unchurched culture, why not design worship that *pleases God?* In other words, why not approach change theologically?

WORSHIP IS CENTRAL

While the focus of this book is not to explore a theology of worship, the assumption that worship is the central purpose of the church undergirds this book. When the apostle John addressed a church threatened by heresy from within and by persecution without, his solution was, "Worship God!" (Rev. 19:10; 22:9), and he set the stage for exalted praise (Rev. 4-5). Again, Paul, the apostle, declares that believers are called to "live to the *praise of his glory*" (Eph. 1:6, 12, 14).

➤ God's Nature Demands Worship

God's very nature demands worship, and his nature is the *motive* driving the changes that touch all areas of church life: relationship building, education, equipping, mentoring, evangelism, programming, staffing, the scheduling of church events, communication styles, architecture, music, and countless other areas. So also, his nature is the *model* for all that we do; our methods must be compatible with the nature of God and what he is doing in people. And, God's nature is also the *measure* of ministry. He has called us to be faithful in glorifying him, not necessarily to be effective in what we think might be good things to do.

➤ Glimpses of God's Glory

Both Paul and John skim the Old Testament Scriptures for themes of transcendence and glimpses of glory. Paul reminds the Corinthians (2 Cor. 3:7-11) of the fading glory of the former days when Moses begged to see God's glory (Exod. 33:12-33) and God said, "You cannot see my face, for no one may see me and live. . . . [but] you will see my back" (Exod. 33:20, 23). Even that indirect glory frightened the people so that Moses covered his face to filter the radiance (Exod. 34). This glory led the children of Israel in pillars of cloud and fire and so flooded the Tent of Meeting that no one dared enter (Exod. 40). Isaiah glimpsed the glory of God in the temple—"the whole earth is full of his glory"(Isa. 6). This vision prompted the prophet's penitence and became both the motive and the measure of his ministry. The tantalizing and terrifying glory of God in the Old Testament "lives in light unapproachable, whom no one has seen or can see" (1 Tim. 6:16).

➤ God's Glory Revealed

However, in the New Testament, Jesus, the Word, who was God, and who created all things, actually "became flesh and made his dwelling among us" (John 1:1-2, 14) and "We have seen his glory, the glory of the One and Only, who came from the Father" (John 1:14). The glory is now refracted into moderated hues that human eyes can behold. Jesus said, "Anyone who has seen me has seen the Father" (John 14:9). The glory once held in light unapproachable now is revealed in observable, comprehensible, trustable, followable, crucifiable form—and we have beheld the glory in the face of Jesus Christ.

➤ God's Glory Reflected by the Church

Paul further says that now the covering which once filtered the terrifying glory has been taken away in Christ (2 Cor. 3:16) so that now we can "with unveiled faces all reflect the Lord's glory" (2 Cor. 3:18). This is the pure essence of worship. Amazingly, we can even change with "ever-increasing glory," into his likeness (2 Cor. 3:18).

This is an overwhelming mega-truth. This means that the glory of God, once held in unapproachable light, then revealed in Jesus Christ, is now actually to be reflected by us in the church! "To him be glory in the church and in Christ Jesus throughout all generations, for ever and ever!" (Eph. 3:21).

➤ The Chief End of Man

There is a sense in which all of life offered in adoration to God and reflecting the glory of God by following Jesus Christ is worship (Rom. 12:1-4). But there is a more specific sense in which the life of worship is driven by the vertical and pure adoration of God, in both private and public. In this vertical adoration, we focus most singularly on God and sensitize ourselves to his majesty, his holiness, his presence, his power, his steadfast love, and his grace.

From this adoration, by his grace and his spirit, flow all other dimensions of the Christian life. As outlined in chapter three, the sequence flows like this: (1) Worship takes us to God. (2) God, in worship, changes lives. (3) Changed lives go forth to nurture relationships and to serve. (4) Authentic relationships and compassionate service underwrite the credibility of evangelism.

Thus, we affirm the Westminster confession of faith when it says, "It is the chief end of man to glorify God and enjoy him forever." We believe that ministry is "to God on behalf of people, not to people on behalf of God."[1] We assume that the central purpose of worship assemblies is not to communicate nor to educate nor to make worshipers feel good nor to impress visitors nor to connect with the unchurched—although to some degree these may all be involved. Rather, the central purpose of worship is to *glorify God*. In worship, God is the audience, not us. The primary purpose is to express authentic adoration to him, not to stir the feelings of the worshiper. God is the one whose feelings and tastes should be pleased, regardless of church constituencies or unchurched target groups.

"WHAT LANGUAGE SHALL I BORROW?"

However—and this must not be ignored—genuine worship must be expressed in the heart language of the worshiper, who will also experience the wonder and joy of praise and adoration. Worship must be intelligible, or it is meaningless. I will sing and pray, as Paul said, "with spirit" and "with understanding" (1 Cor. 14:15—ASV). Worship must be heartfelt or it is vain. As Rubel Shelly said, "If worship is not relevant, it is not biblical."

Now, after this all too brief excursion into theology, (sources for further study are listed in the appendixes) we return to the central theme of this book: *change*—the need for change, and the practical dynamics of navigating through change. But I am only interested in the kind of change that is motivated and measured by the heart and the will of God!

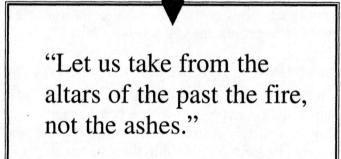

"Let us take from the altars of the past the fire, not the ashes."

$\mathcal{L}$IFE SPANS:
Respecting the Past

An elder friend recently suggested that we should levy a fine of one dollar every time any person in our church used the word *change*. Change is a scary word, loaded with tons of troubling baggage, maybe for some surprising reasons. We may be singing a negative perspective into our subconscious. One of my favorite hymns is "Abide With Me," written by Henry F. Lyte. However, in one of the lines, my friend Henry did a number on us: "Change and decay in all around I see . . ." Result? Somewhere beneath the waterline of consciousness, many a good ol' hymn-singing believer harbors a powerful negative reaction to the word "change," which is unfortunate! To me, Henry Lytes's line is an oxymoron. Change and decay do not belong together. Death and decay are bed-fellows. Change belongs with life and vitality. In fact, re-sponsible change may be one of the most hopeful words for the future vitality of our fellowship. These winds may well be blowing us a breath of spring!

The word change carries negative baggage for another reason, too. When we talk about change at church, it sounds like disloyalty to our heritage; it appears to be crit-icism of traditional and older churches and their leaders. I confess, I'm hungry for change, but by now I hope you sense that I see change as *building* on our past, not de-stroying it.

OF PERSONS AND PARISHES

Look at it this way: When my father was a young man, he was known far and wide in our Canadian homestead district as a man of unusual physical strength and speed. He also possessed a winsome personality. I well remem-ber the year my dad turned forty. The neighbors surprised him with a birthday party and gave him a new rocking chair. They reminisced about kindnesses Dad had shown to this one and that. They dusted off old legends about Dad's physical strength when he was young, of how much he could lift and how fast he could run. Even when I was fourteen and on the track team and Dad was forty-four, he could still beat me in a fifty-yard dash. Of course, all ac-knowledged my dad as an attentive and tender father.

We lost Dad the day before Christmas in 1991. The winds of eighty-five winters had whitened his hair, weath-ered his face, and withered his body. Things had really changed. Dad hadn't fathered any babies in five decades. He couldn't run any more, and he could scarcely lift a feather. Cancer had slowed him to a feeble walk during his last year, leading finally to a stroke. In those final weeks Dad was partly paralyzed and couldn't even talk. But in spite of his frailty and immobility, Dad was still enormously valuable and important to me and to a lot of other people. I wasn't the least bit embarrassed that he'd quit having children and slowed down physically. Of course not. Dad had long since passed life's season for those kinds of things. With unfolding years my father had simply moved through the changing roles most appropriate to each season of his life. But each advancing role was still authentic and to be valued. He grew older. Finally he died, as is the common lot of humankind.

CHURCHES' LIFE CYCLES

Churches are like people in some ways. Both have life spans. Both are born and both grow old. Some live longer than others, but they eventually die.

Robert Dale, in his books *To Dream Again* and *Keeping the Dream Alive,*[1] tracks the life cycle of churches on a bell curve—birth–growth–maturity–decline–death. His research shows that the average life span for churches in this country is less than eighty years. The ones that live past that, he says, usually become "pastor killers." Only a few find "new phases of vitality"; they might relocate or through changing circumstance have a complete turnover of people. The average zenith of growth and vitality for a church is usually somewhere between year seventeen and year twenty-seven. The circumstances in the urban area around the church usually determine the cycle of the church. A neighborhood booms; its churches, if healthy, boom. A neighborhood declines; its churches decline. A neighborhood changes; its churches sometimes change, but more often, die. Look around you. Dale is right.

Of course, with some churches, decline can be traced more to internal factors than to changing communities. Historically, we have all seen churches die in the midst of vital and stable communities. Actually, fewer than 5 percent adjust, turn around, and grow again by healthy outreach. Usually, such cases require some skillful turn-around management. So observes Dale. But, of course, no technique can replace the power of God nor can any skill save a church if God withdraws his hand from it.

Also, churches, like people, tend to fill a certain function at one season of life and another function at the next season, as the developmental stages unfold. This is normal. But—mark this down—like persons, churches are no less valuable and authentic at one stage of life than the other, just different.

Just because some older or more traditional congregations may not be able to change enough to connect with the mainstream of current American culture, does not mean we should write them off. Doing so is both wrongheaded and wrong-hearted. Older, more traditional churches have authentic roles, and many are of enormous value even though, in their later life, they do not look or perform the same as they did in their youth. Remember that of all churches in America twenty-five years old and older, more than 80 percent are plateaued or in decline and fewer than 5 percent are growing by evangelizing the unchurched. But think this through. Young churches, like young people, tend to be more aggressive and have high energy. They are usually growth-oriented, single-minded, vision-driven, experimental, flexible, and dynamic.

As churches age, however, and add layers of constituencies, they tend to become less goal-oriented, less evangelistic, less focused and vision-driven. Their purposes may shift. For example, when churches slow down and quit producing "babies," they may become stabilizers, nurturers, senders, and supporters. But don't ask them to run the evangelistic sprint or the church-growth marathon. And don't expect flexible experimentation or quick change any more than you would have expected it from my father at eighty-five. Nor does this mean that, in their later stages, these churches are less Christian or less valuable to God and to others simply because they haven't produced many converts lately.

No, I'm not suggesting that individual Christians ever become exempt from caring about lost people. But *groups* of Christians (churches) do become less aggressive as they get older. Nor is it always tragic when churches, having completed their life cycle, die! If and when one congregation ages and dies, however, it is not an indication that our whole movement is dying. Some old churches will be able to change approaches, reconnect with the culture, and grow again. Meanwhile, we must be planting some new, young churches that look, dress, and perform differently from their parents—churches that will reach the unchurched of our constantly changing world. A cycle of the birth–growth–decline–death of local congregations describes the life stream of the church from Pentecost on—and likely will till the end of time. The same cycle is the life stream of all living things.

IN THE SPIRIT OF OUR FOREFATHERS

My sons loved their grandfather. They saw him to be both important and valuable at each stage of his life, even toward the end when he lay paralyzed and unable even to talk. However, if my boys had become so enamored with their grandfather that they imitated everything about him, I might have grown alarmed. If they had dressed in the styles of the twenties and adopted his vocabulary and lifestyle, they would have become social oddities (and wouldn't likely produce any babies, because no girls their age would marry such eccentrics!). And if they mimicked Granddad's education (less than sixth grade) they would perish in our kind of world.

The fact that my kids did not imitate Dad's times and his culture surely cannot be construed as disrespect for him. And to call for changes in the church does not imply disrespect for the past either. Call me a change agent, but don't ask me to declare open season on our heritage. The current generation of Christians was nurtured in churches built a long time ago and at great cost.

Scores of preachers spent their lifetimes building up churches without ever having the assurance of a regular salary. Some were paid for their time in fresh farm produce. (Joe Blue of Arkansas is said to have trudged wearily home from at least one evangelistic trip lugging a live pig under his arm.) We're deeply indebted to those people. And I love the churches they planted. Most of those pioneers devised creative and innovative strategies to connect with the culture they were trying to reach. Frankly, they did a much better job reaching their culture than we're doing in reaching ours! But, we are showing no respect for them by clinging nostalgically to the methods and strategies that worked for them, if, in so doing, we fail to reach the unchurched of our times.

Former strategies, methods, forms, customs, and vocabulary cannot be imitated in our day with effectiveness. They do not fit our times and were not meant to. Let's remember our religious forebears with affectionate nostalgia. Good sense says we need our roots. But when we wake up tomorrow morning, it will not be 1870, nor 1950. Not even 1980. And working harder at outmoded forms, methods, and strategies will not produce more success— only more frustration! In the spirit of our forefathers, we must devise strategies that connect with our place and time. And we must continue to learn honestly from Scripture, allowing our beliefs to progress with every new insight into God's word.

Yes! Of course we must change significantly to remain true to Scripture and to reach major segments of our culture, even to keep our own children. But then, is change anything new?

WHAT ON EARTH IS "CHURCH"?

> Oh, look! Here comes the apostle Paul riding up Central Boulevard on a donkey and looking for the church.
>
> "Well," we explain, "there is the church at the corner of Fifth and Highland, and the Madison church, and Richland Hills, and . . ."
>
> Paul's eyes widen, "What are the brethren doing there?"
>
> "Oh," we explain again, "that is where the buildings are."
>
> "Buildings?"

"Church buildings, of course."

Paul leans forward with curiosity, "What is a church building?"

"Where the pews are, and the pulpit."

"What are those?"

"Well, the pews are where the people sit when the communion trays are passed," we answer.

"And what are communion trays?" asks our bewildered apostle.

This line of talk is getting us nowhere, so we shift directions: "The song leader stands in the pulpit and . . ."

"What is a song leader?"

"He opens the hymnbook and leads us in praise before we go to our classes in the educational wing."

Poor Paul doesn't seem to understand church at all. "And what are hymnbooks, classes, and educational wings?"

This guided tour rambles on as we lead Paul through explanations of the baptistry, the foyer, the nursery, the fellowship hall, youth ministry, vacation Bible school, gospel meetings, etc., describing "church," or at least what we think of when we think of church. We definitely do not want these "church" elements changed! What we're really describing, however, is actually only one way to do church—one cultural expression of the church—designed primarily for nineteenth century rural America. Paul knows it is not how church was done in New Testament times, nor is it designed to "connect" in mainstream, urban U.S.A. in 1994.

WHERE IS THE "PATTERN"?

But, someone asks, does not the Bible describe an eternal and universal pattern for the church? Well, yes and no.

No, the New Testament does not blueprint one way of expressing the church to be bound in all times and in all cultures.

Yes, the Bible describes how church was done, but in many different ways and fitted to a variety of cultural settings. The large gatherings in Jerusalem looked very different from the house churches of Rome. In Ephesus, Paul taught in a school; in Athens, at the town square. The church on Crete was scattered among rural and village settings on a remote island quite unlike the sophisticated urban Ephesus. Even the list of qualities for elders was different for Crete (Titus 1) than for Ephesus (1 Tim. 3). The two cultural settings call for different leadership skills and qualities.

And Paul's preaching strategy was far different in Athens—where he quoted pagan poets, from his preaching in Jewish settings—where he appealed to the Old Testament. Timothy is required to be circumcised in one setting (Acts 16:3), while the church is forbidden to circumcise Titus in another (Gal. 2:3-5).

Change is written all over the New Testament! In fact, the very message of the gospel calls us to become a "new creation" (2 Cor. 5:17).

Earlier, we mentioned that negatively loaded reference to "change and decay" in Henry F. Lyte's hymn "Abide With Me." In spite of the oxymoron, that hymn remains one of my favorites. I especially cherish the line: "Oh, Thou who changest not, abide with me."

He wills the ever changing forms of our future, although he himself remains the same yesterday, today, and forever.

WHAT MUST SURELY CHANGE

"I have become all things to all men so that by all possible means I might save some."
1 Corinthians 9:22

"If worship is not relevant, it is not biblical."
—Rubel Shelly[1]

Back in the mid 1800s, church leaders were not only in *touch* with culture, they were *creating* it!

A CHURCH THAT CONNECTS

Back in the mid 1800s, when churches were spreading across the plains at exploding rates, church leaders were not only in *touch* with the culture, they were *creating* it! But we solidified these gains, settled on our turf, and made old styles and strategies sacred, while the culture moved on. We were left in the wake, and now we find ourselves fighting with each other about whether or not we ought to catch up again, and if so, how? And what exactly will this renewed, changed, culturally updated church look like? I cannot tell you specifically, unless you tell me a lot about where this church is located and who it wants to reach.

Its working *vocabulary* will vary from place to place. For example, as we apply the gospel, academic language may fit well in a college community, business jargon in an urban boomer community, or the nomenclature of the factory in an industrial community.

The *musical idiom* in this church that connects will match the heart language of the people. Congregational singing of classical hymns from books, directed by one song leader may fit some settings, while using an overhead projector to display contemporary music, led by a worship team (with occasional special solos or groups) may fit in another.

Traditional Sunday morning Bible classes might work well in one place, while Sunday evening home Bible studies might work better in another. Off-site learning experiences on different nights of the week may work better in yet another, while drama may communicate well in other settings.

The church of the future may wear a number of different faces. And its expression will likely change from year to year. It may dress in many things, and in our changing culture, it may need to update its wardrobe constantly.

All across North America, new churches are springing up. Churches that do connect with our culture. Churches that are growing! One of these began sixteen years ago with less than forty people and has grown to Sunday assemblies of over fourteen thousand. Another began with two people thirteen years ago but now has over five thousand members—and has started over twenty-five daughter churches. And there are many others. In fact, news media have reported that at least one thousand such rapid-growth churches now exist in America.[2]

By no means do all these churches look alike. They look as different from each other as the communities where they are planted. They use a variety of methods, strategies, and formats; but certain common principles run through all of them.

➤ Growing churches put strong trust in prayer and the Holy Spirit.

Of course, all churches pray, but effective, growing churches are actually founded upon and driven by heart-felt prayer. If we buy into the notion that some flashy new technique will make us personal evangelists or some mysterious new education media or small group configuration will automatically create growing disciples, or that tinkering with lights and microphones and choreography will create worshipers, we are barking up the wrong tree! God is the only one who can grow churches. Only the Spirit of God can change the human heart. I cannot convert anyone. Neither can you. Even when we do "all the right things," if God is not in them, whatever results will be phantom gains.

Good news! In hundreds of congregations across our land God is awakening a new spirit of prayer. At one church, every Sunday morning, while the preacher is standing in the pulpit, upwards of a hundred people are circled in an adjacent room praying that God will use that message and that hour of worship. We are witnessing something of this prayer revival at my home congregation, Preston Road Church of Christ. People are studying prayer; books on prayer and worship quickly evaporate from our book table. And people are praying. Eighteen months ago, the whole congregation participated in the selection of eight new elders. Months of focused prayer preceded the selection process. Living rooms are often full of Christians gathered to pray on behalf of the sick. A core of Christians gathers to pray for me every Sunday before I step into the pulpit. Small groups keep evangelistic prayer lists and meet to report answered prayer. Of course, we are by no means the only church experiencing this. This revival of prayer passion seems to be nationwide. Praise God!

"Seekers" feel drawn to churches that expect God to act. In these days when people are glutted on technology and jaded by futility, they are not going to take a church seriously that does not take the supernatural seriously.

➤ Churches that connect have positive leadership.

First, positive leadership is *led,* not driven. It follows a vision, a call, a conviction, rather than running from a problem. Leaders who get mad and pull out—"I'll take my marbles and start my own game"—are not positive leaders, and God will not bless their efforts! Such "walk-out" churches rarely amount to much! They attract malcontents and eccentrics and tend to feed on a theology of "here's-what's-wrong-with-where-we-came-from and ain't-we-glad-we're-not-like-them-any-more." Most walk-out churches do not survive, and those that do tend to be small, joyless, and stagnant. This writer wants nothing to do with such negative leadership. Michelangelo may have said it best for me, "I criticize by creating something beautiful."

Second, positive leadership means individuals gifted with strong visionary leadership are released to lead! A scan of history shows that every time God made a major move among his people, he used persons with special gifts of leadership: Abraham, Ruth, Esther, Moses, Joshua, Deborah, John the Baptist, Aquila, Paul, Zwingli, Luther, Campbell, Stone—visionaries, change agents!

Visionaries aren't always preachers. For example, the Richland Hills Church of Christ, in the Fort Worth, Texas, area, is a leading growth story among Churches of Christ. Although, they have been led by a string of great preachers, their charge was led by a visionary elder, Bill New. Today's growing churches sense the people whom God has gifted with vision—whether they be elders, preachers, deacons, women, whoever they are—and empower them to draw maps into the twenty-first century.

> **Effective churches usually have a clear purpose and vision statement.**

One dad tells about attending his son's first soccer game. The boys had a great time playing the game, but no one on his son's team scored a goal. Dad said, "Son, how come you didn't try to score any goals?"

To which his son replied, "What's a goal, Dad?"

Formulating a purpose statement is figuring out what the goal is and communicating it clearly. George Barna says, "Perhaps the single, most important factor that describes a user friendly church is the presence of God's vision for the ministry of the church. Without it, you cannot have a user friendly church."[3] Not many churches have such a clear vision. A major reason churches twenty-five years old and older are not growing is that they have collected layers of constituencies who have "joined" at various eras. Each constituency has its own vision of what the church is about. Thus, attempts by any one group to mount a militant mission are neutralized by the other constituencies. And, to borrow (and misuse) a saying from Scripture, "Where there is no vision, the people perish." (The passage literally reads: "When no prophet receives a message from God, the people are without guidance.")

Someone said, "A good purpose statement is big enough to keep you busy for a lifetime, yet small enough to fit on a bumper sticker." This is likely a gross oversimplification, but you get the point. For example, during the 1980s, the in-house purpose statement of the Lanier Copy corporation was only two words: "Bury Xerox." Simple, but eloquent. And every department understood the implications.

Actually, purpose statements generally emerge on three levels: *values*—what you believe in, your presuppositions; *mission*—what you are trying to accomplish and with whom; and *strategy*—the way you are going to get it done. The congregation I preach for has spelled out that first level of values. "It is the purpose of the Preston Road Church of Christ to glorify God by doing the will of Jesus Christ, in the power of the Holy Spirit." That is what we value.

Our guns are loaded with the values. Now we are attempting a mission statement—at what target will we aim those guns? Then next we will devise strategies to accomplish our mission. Our congregation is fifty-three years old and has many "layers." Thus, getting the constituencies aligned is a slow and demanding process, but the results could shake our city.

➤ **Churches that connect with the culture will target a specific people.**

Targeting is a bit controversial because, at first blush, "targeting" sounds like excluding those not on the bull's eye. But in actuality, one church cannot reach all kinds of people. If it tries to, it won't be effective in reaching any people. A church that "connects" will specialize in the kind of people it can reach best. Of course, all kinds of people are welcome and all are precious to Jesus. But, remember, God himself commissioned Peter and Paul for two distinctly different "target" groups. Peter targeted Jews; Paul, the Gentiles. Thus, their strategies, assumptions, and vocabulary were different.

Let me illustrate targeting in a modern, urban setting: The church in Dallas, where I minister, is located in the Park Cities, an affluent and prestigious old-money community. Last year we planted a daughter church, the Central Dallas Church of Christ, in east Dallas, one of the poorest and most troubled sections of town. Carey Dowl, the gifted and passionate preacher for that new plant, understands clearly that inner-city people will not likely be reached from a Park Cities congregation. Besides, Carey is black, and thus many of the people of east Dallas trust him more easily than they would a Caucasian, especially a Caucasian from the Park Cities. Carey also understands that "targeting" Central Dallas means that an inner-city church must look very different from the Preston Road church. Perhaps the point is made more dramatically by standing the situation on its head. Think how difficult it would be to begin a church in east Dallas, with east Dallas people for the purpose of reaching people in the Park Cities!

No one church can serve everybody. Each congregation must decide who it wants to serve. Growing churches draw a bull's eye so they know what to shoot at.

Targeting churches listen to the community. They ask questions. Some do it very simply by asking, "Do you go to a church?" If the answer is no, then they ask, "What kind of church would you go to?" Once they form a profile of the people in their community, they simply program to meet the needs of the target group. They plan the church not for the "old timers," but for the specific unchurched people they are trying to reach.

➢ Growing churches avoid needless turnoffs and plan attractive and user-friendly assemblies.

They plan assemblies that will make sense to their target community. They make it easy for guests to find their way into the assemblies. They also generate a warm, friendly, and contemporary environment. They speak the message in language that makes sense to the uninitiated. In modern urban settings, these churches avoid abstract, antiquated, religious jargon.

They use music that connects with the heart language of the target culture. They assume that "if we don't connect with music, we do not connect!" (Chapter 9 will explore music further.)

Assemblies of growing churches use contemporary media as well. For example, when pleasant, attractive, current-looking slides flash words on a screen and simple, contemporary melodies are led by folks that look like people the guests might have seen somewhere besides church, the uninitiated urbanite can more easily relate. In

short, assemblies of growing churches make every effort
to narrow the cultural gap from their world to the church.

➢ **User-friendly churches employ educational approaches that fit the learning style of the people they
are trying to reach.**

For example, Carey Dowl would not think of having a
two-hour seminar on hermeneutics on six successive
Thursday nights in east Dallas. We have offered this kind
of seminar in the Park Cities (but, even then, specifically
with belonging believers in mind). But such an approach
would not connect in the inner city. First, hermeneutics is
not a burning issue in the inner city. Second, seminars and
classes are not the learning style of unchurched inner-city
people. They are hands-on people who learn best by mentoring and on-the-job training.

➢ **Effective churches may have two kinds of assemblies.**

Many growing churches have two styles of Sunday
morning worship services: one contemporary worship
service and another traditional. This is helpful in older
churches, especially in an effort to keep young people
participating. However, when starting a church from
scratch, two different worship assemblies would divide
your target.

A word of caution, however: Two types of services can
easily polarize into the "good Christians" and the "bad
Christians" or "the old fogies" and "the young smart-
alecks." However, in some congregations two kinds of
worship services have been an excellent strategy. For example the Highland Street Church of Christ in Memphis,
Tennessee, is an old church in an excellent growth mode.
They have two relatively traditional worship assemblies

in the "sanctuary" and one "contemporary" assembly in the family-life center. In spite of mild tension, they appear to be transitioning effectively.

However, most churches that connect have a *worship* service for Christians and an *outreach* service for seekers (a term commonly used for the receptive nonchurched). They see a clear distinction between the needs of worshipers and the needs of seekers. For example, you might bring a friend to church for the first time and the preacher holds forth on something ethereal like "The History of the Doctrine of Predestination" and asks the audience to "follow in their Bibles" while he jumps all over the centuries. Your guest would likely feel a combination of bewilderment, intimidation, and boredom. Seekers need Christianity 101—simple message, practical, and user friendly. Rather than congregational singing of hymns from books, a seeker's service might have one or two very simple and singable congregational songs, with words projected on a screen. Since guests are often intimidated by being expected to sing, the rest of the music might be contemporary songs presented by a small singing group (not a choir; choir music won't likely connect either). Today's music culture is a listening culture.

Story has it that a man from the Midwest designed a hybrid vehicle—it was at the same time an automobile and an aircraft. Fly it to your city of choice. Land. Detach the wings and store them in a little trailer. Then drive the thing around town until time to unpack your trailer, spread your wings, and fly back home. The idea bombed for two reasons: It wasn't a good car and it wasn't a good airplane. In a similar sense, trying to evangelize the nonchurched and nurture the saints in the same assembly often misses one crowd or the other—sometimes both.

For this reason a number of churches have assemblies at a point in the week when they find seekers most likely to attend, and they teach Christianity 101, using the kind of media, vocabulary, and style that fit the seeker. Then, at another time in the week, Christians meet for thirty-five to forty minutes of expository preaching and thirty-five to forty minutes of praise. Growing Christians feed on word and worship, which would overload the circuits of seekers straight off the streets.

> **Effective growing churches don't back away from a strong biblical message, but present it in user-friendly language.**

God is building an army, not merely gathering an audience. Jesus aims to build Christians, not just to bring a crowd. In many (not all) of the growing churches, the preacher simply opens the Bible week after week and works through books of the Bible—diving deep in the assembly of the saints, but staying simpler in the seeker's service. The most effective churches do their strongest Bible teaching in small groups where they hold each other accountable—not just to learn but to obey. Some churches offer advanced Bible classes and seminars at various points of the calendar.

However, the *language* of the biblical teaching is user friendly. The Bible is the most relevant book in history, but not if it is exegeted into the air and left floating somewhere over people's heads. Effective teaching zip-codes Scripture to real people.

➤ Effective churches lead people through some form of user-friendly assimilation track.

Seekers and visitors can easily find their way into growing churches. Serious inquirers come to church wanting relationships, wanting to grow, and longing to be "difference makers." So they are looking for training and guidance. But each visitor must begin his or her growth journey at his or her level and travel at his or her own speed. This will not likely happen if the uninitiated are rushed into classrooms full of longtime Christians who are rerunning Romans for the twelfth time and where members talk mostly to each other.

In spite of this, most congregations currently have woefully inadequate assimilating tracks. Many congregations have no such infrastructure to involve members. Other churches have plenty of infrastructure, maintained for two purposes: (1) To keep longtime members happy, and (2) to maintain control. Consequently, even if we attract a lot of visitors to a church where people are friendly and worship is uplifting, a few months later, we lose a lot of them. They grow bored with just coming to church. Persistent and discerning newcomers may eventually find their way in, but in most churches, many don't. In my own congregation, for example, literally hundreds have passed through our midst this year whom we never guided to help, hope, and home. Growing churches, however, know exactly how they will pick up each person at the door and lead him or her step by step, stage by stage toward spiritual maturity.

The good news is that things are changing! In our congregation, as in many others, a force of bright and committed people is constructing what they have termed, "a user-friendly track, from the street through the heart of the church to the throne."

➤ User-friendly churches offer hands-on guidance to personalized ministry.

This may well be the most important thing for Church of Christ people to learn from other growing, user-friendly churches. If I were to prioritize the urgent changes needed in Churches of Christ today, I would put this at the top of the list. Yes, worship needs attention, and we need user-friendly assemblies. And while those are crucially important, what we need even more is to equip individual people to do the kind of ministry God has gifted them to do. This means: First, help them discover their spiritual gifts; second, help them select their ministry; and third, give them personal, hands-on training to go and do that ministry.

Leaders take note: When the Bible most specifically spells out the task of spiritual leaders, it clearly identifies that task as "preparing God's people for works of service" (Eph. 4:12). When church leaders neglect this, to that degree they fail in their God-given calling and role. And to that degree, we will continue to circulate inquiring people in the front door and out the back door of our churches.

➤ Growing churches intentionally staff for growth.

In growing churches, staff budgets are spent on people who have skill to help new folks find their gifts and to teach them how to get involved in ministry. The function of staff is not to *do* ministry; it is to equip or empower every Christian to do his or her ministry. In our fast-moving, competitive times, volunteer leaders simply cannot be expected to have the time or the skills to recruit, equip, nurture, organize, and cycle people for ministry. (Some people label this process with the acronym, RENOC.) A church will usually stop growing a few months after it stops adding effective staff. Lyle Schaller says for a church to be staffed to grow, it must add a staff person for every one hundred members.[4] This specific ratio may be questioned, but churches that grow are churches that staff for growth.

➤ **Effective, growing churches tolerate diversity in nonessentials.**

However, being tolerant does not imply compromising on the essential issues of the faith. What are the "essentials"? For lists of the "essentials" and "nonessentials," you will have to consult someone much wiser than I. I have noticed that list differs from one locality to another. For example, when I grew up in Canada, our church held as one of its essentials that Christians must not attend Hollywood movies. However, we loved water. We had much more water than could be found, for example, in West Texas. However, in those days in parts of Texas, males and females were not allowed to swim together. They called that "mixed bathing." When Texas youth groups would come up to Canada to help with summer VBS, we developed a tug-of-war over Sunday afternoon activities. In the early afternoon, we went to the lake. The Canadian kids swam, while the Texas kids sat in the cars doing things they shouldn't, but feeling righteous because they were not "mixed bathing." In the late afternoons, we went downtown. The Texas kids watched the movies, while the Canadian kids sat in the cars, doing things they shouldn't, but feeling righteous because they were not "poisoning their minds with Hollywood harlots and salacious sluts" (as one preacher used to explain it). Since most of our urban communities nowadays are somewhat cosmopolitan, several theological "geographies" from Alabama to Afghanistan to Alberta often show up under one congregational roof, so growing churches must learn how to be tolerant in nonessentials.

➤ **Effective churches focus on genuine relationships.**

The first relationship: The beginning point for all Christians must be a personal relationship with Christ. The objective of growing churches is to build a body of devoted followers of Christ.

A second relationship: Relationship with Christ is nurtured through relationships with the people of Christ. Today's urban people are often estranged from each other, even afraid of each other. Folks out there on the street are looking for something: help, hope, and home—help in dealing with their problems; hope that life has some kind of meaning or purpose for them and that they can "make a difference"; and home, a place to belong, to put down their roots.

As we've said before, for a church to get bigger it's got to get smaller. But small groups and meaningful relationships won't happen automatically. They require intentional focus and planning. Generous chunks of staff energy and time is necessary to (RENOC) recruit, equip, nurture, organize, and cycle small group leaders.

A third relationship: Effective churches encourage their people to build authentic relationships with nonchurched people, people outside of Christ. Research

across the last two decades repeatedly observes that more
than 80 percent of people who become believers and
members of a given congregation do so through the influence of a friend or a relative. There is no magic to this.
Jesus conducted his ministry through relationships. He
spent three years nurturing intimate relationships with
twelve people and equipping them for ministry. His parting word to them was, "Now, you guys, go do that with
others." Paul passed on this principle, too. He modeled it,
always traveling with an entourage of Timothys. He artic-
ulated it as well: "The things you have heard me say
. . . entrust to reliable men . . . who will also be qualified
to teach others" (2 Tim. 2:2). Evangelism in growing
churches generally doesn't rely on extravagant public advertising. They do their evangelism through authentic relationships. This means rank and file members are given
high ownership in personal evangelism.

Evangelism is not viewed as an event, but as a process.
Even follow-up with visitors is most effectively carried
out by the person who brought that visitor. Thus, in growing and effective churches, ministers and leaders system-
atically equip individual Christians to witness to their
friends and to follow-up. User-friendly churches recruit,
equip, nurture, organize, and cycle, volunteer personal
witnesses. Dr. Jim Samuel, one of the elders of our congregation, works like "yeast in dough" to train all in our
congregation to be able to "give their testimony," to tell
their own story about what God has done for them. That
is "quintessential shepherding." Someone is doing this in
some form in every effective church!

➤ **Finally, churches that connect are intentional.**

Intentionality simply means intent, purpose, functioning by objective. A key, operative question for intentional churches is, "Is the thing we are doing right now accomplishing our purpose?"

Remember how strategies became events, events became traditions, and finally traditions became dogma. One strategy that became event is the Sunday night evangelistic service. Back in the early 1800s when gas lights were first introduced across the west, people would stream in from the country on Sunday nights to see these newfangled lights. Preachers turned those ready-made crowds into mini-revivals. This kicked off the idea of Sunday night services, which spread to become standard practice across much of the country. It worked wonderfully for decades back then and there. But not in urban America in 1994. Yet we are still holding Sunday night services, even though our people are scattered over the city. Few members attend, let alone nonchurched people. What was once an excellent strategy became simply an expected event. This practice has lost its intentionality. Ask yourself, "Why are people not coming to the building on Sunday nights in our urban church?" Usually because it is merely an expected event, rather than a useful strategy that intentionally and effectively accomplishes a specific purpose.

One clear clue to the loss of intentionality, for example, is when the educational committee scratches its collective head and ponders, "Now let's see. What shall we study this quarter on Wednesday nights?" What that really means is, "We don't know what we are trying to accomplish with Wednesday night classes." The assumption is,

"We are doing this to get a crowd. So, let's study something that will bring folks out." Why get a crowd, if for no purpose? Intentionality would ask, "How do our Wednesday nights help accomplish our purpose?" If Wednesday night meetings accomplish no purpose, why have them? When the horse is dead, dismount.

Now, wait a minute! Our point is not that we should disband Sunday night and Wednesday night gatherings. Not at all. But if we are going to expend that much time and energy—and ask hundreds of others to pack up their families and drag them across the city two nights per week—let's make double-sure these practices are serving a key purpose. If they are not, like all meaningless, energy-draining projects, either change them or drop them! Effective churches cannot afford to squander precious limited hours, dollars, or human resources on meaningless activity. Intentionality asks over and over, "Is this taking us where we want to go?"

But, we are learning! We are moving toward being churches that connect—purposeful, user-friendly, spirit-empowered congregations! Like the men of Issachar, are we learning to "understand the times so we will know what to do?" (1 Chron. 12:32). We are beginning to see that there is no inherent reason why older, aligned churches cannot reach people with the amazing effectiveness that we see among many young Bible churches and community churches. And we are learning that to do this we must change—significantly! The future is going to be even better, as we observe much, learn more, work smarter, network with each other, and pray without ceasing. Like our forefathers in 1860, we are learning how to be a church that connects. I sing in the shower thinking about what is ahead. Oh, yes, we can—we will—walk our way through the fresh winds of change!

Besides screening right-brained people from our churches, we may have wrung the right-brain juices from our Bibles.

RIGHT-BRAINED CHRISTIANS IN A LEFT-BRAINED CHURCH

After class, Pat pulled me aside, "Could I talk with you. I'm feeling hurt and a bit offended." Tears welled up in her eyes as Pat went on, "I felt as if you were putting down the past. Or my parents. Or something. And I feel, well, uncomfortable.

"I was raised to believe that we worship God 'decently and orderly' with our minds. Emotionalism was dangerous. But what we just did in class was so different! I do feel something in that kind of worship. But I get scared when I feel things in church. I can go to a movie or a concert or dancing to get my emotional high. Can't we keep emotion out of church? But then, I guess I resent leaving part of myself out of church too."

Pat speaks for a lot of us.

A STUDY OF CONTRASTS

The class which triggered Pat's comments was one in which our worship team helped me contrast two styles of worship: one designed for "thinker" people (left-brainers), the other for "feeler" people (right-brainers). I had explained that our right brain houses our creative activities and the left brain the analytical abilities and that stereotypes of left-brainers include accountants, computer whizzes, surgeons, scientists, and scholars, while the stereotypical right-brainer is an artist, a musician, a poet, or a preacher. Speaking in generalities, one style of worship fits thinkers and another style fits feelers.

Since the fellowship of which I am a part is heavily left-brained and rationalistic in its emphasis and style, I wanted the class to experience both styles of worship as well as discuss them. So we kicked off segment one with three traditional hymns from the old hymnbook. Jeff, our song leader, led from up front, warmly but very formally, traditionally. After each song he double-announced the next number. No two hymns were on the same theme.

Then Robert read Scripture (on yet another subject) in traditional style. Next followed an impromptu prayer, which, while not meant to be that way, turned out to be trite and impersonal, probably because it was led by a last-minute recruit. Left-brained people were feeling secure and at home. Things were familiar and heavily cerebral. I assume their worship was genuine. Right-brained people, however, fiddled with pew racks, counted ceiling tiles, and checked their watches.

Between the first and second segments, I explained, "Both thinkers and feelers were created by God. Neither are good/bad or right/wrong. God simply wired us up differently."

All of us have both feeler and thinker in us. But according to demographer George Barna, 45 percent of us are dominantly right-brained, 45 percent dominantly left-brained, and 10 percent more equally feeler/thinker.[1]

In segment two, the tempo of the class shifted abruptly into celebrative praise and worship, with contemporary songs projected on a screen in colorful graphics. Readings, prayers, and singing clustered around a single theme. The worship team led directly from one song to the next without interruption, intentionally moving the tone and content of worship in a specific direction, gathering the congregation into the momentum of the experience. A few songs included clapping and one or two worshipers actually "lifted holy hands." The beaming expressions of the worship leaders spread to the class members.

Several short Scripture readings moved quickly from one reader to the next, climaxing in a congregational responsive reading. When we knelt for prayer, several people prayed poignantly about specific real-life issues, the prayers were interspersed with periods of silence. The feeler/creative right-brainers were transported while some thinker/analytical left-brainers rolled their eyes, and their body language said, "Oh, please! Give me a break!"

In the third segment, I taught twenty minutes on "Hindrances to Worship: Overemphasizing Our Rational Selves." We analyzed the contrasting styles of worship we had just experienced and why some responded better to one style and some to another. Drawing from Paul's "all things to all men" theme (1 Cor. 9:22), I called upon both right- and left-brained personalities to lovingly celebrate our diversity, because:

1. God is the one who designed us.
2. The praise of half our people might be inhibited if we hold exclusively to one style of worship or the other.
3. If feelers (right-brainers) are to worship in their heart language, our assemblies may need to include more experiential and celebrative ingredients, but not to the exclusion of more cerebral elements.
4. To worship in the heart language of the young, we may need to include contemporary formats, without scrapping all the traditional.
5. And, if our assemblies are to connect with visitors who are not acculturated to our traditional, stained-glass, and left-brain liturgy, we must avoid in-house, churchy vocabulary and musical styles.

MIXED REVIEWS

As Pat and I examined mixed reactions to the class, she explained:

"I understand 'right-brain/left-brain' stuff. I'm a school teacher trained in learning styles. In fact, I'm right-brained myself. I teach art, for goodness sake! And I crave right-brain experiences, music, and drama; but . . ."

Pat's next comment spoke worlds of truth and hit a nerve with me! But let me interrupt Pat one more time to visit a moment with Cheryl.

Cheryl is part of a second category of right-brained Christians. She is one of the thousands who have left our fellowship because they feel that "something" is missing. Months after she had left, Cheryl visited over breakfast with the minister from her old home church.

"When I left, I didn't know precisely what I wanted, though I searched for 'it' in a number of churches. But I think I've put my finger on 'it,'" Cheryl explained. "In my home church we always talked about Jesus in the past tense—New Testament times. But in the churches that connect with my spirit, Jesus occupies the present tense—connected to now! I hungered to experience personal relationship with God. Now! Not just talk about someone else's experience with him two thousand years ago."

Swarms of Cheryls leave our left-brained fellowships every year.

Jack represents a third group: right-brainers outside our fellowship who want God and who study the Bible. Some of them do check us out, but most don't come back. No, we're not unfriendly or insincere. Right-brained people just find it hard to connect with a left-brained church.

Jack is one of these. Jack makes his living playing in a band with Richard, who led Jack to Christ through personal Bible study. Richard said, "Jack fell in love with Jesus at first sight and loved the idea of being 'just a Christian.' But when Jack visited Old Paths Church with me, things didn't go so well for Jack's right-brained musician's temperament. Worship that particular day ran off the charts into 'left-brain analytical,' and our church is already an unusually cerebral kind of church, even on the most exciting days."

After church, Jack smiled politely and told Richard, "Thanks for the invite. Nice folks here, but Old Paths Church is not really my cup of tea. If I start going to church regularly it will likely be down at New Song Community Chapel. Things *feel* better there."

Every member of Richard's band eventually came to Christ and visited Old Paths with Richard. None of them stayed there. Mike, a strong left-brainer who overheard Jack's comments, wrote off Jack and his friends as merely wanting to get a "buzz" out of church rather than wanting to worship God. Possibly. But God made both men. And Jack's expresser-feeler heart language is just as God-designed for God-honoring worship as is Mike's cerebral-analytical left-brain style.

HOW WE LEARNED TO LEAN LEFT

But Mike is not alone. As a fellowship, we noninstrumental Churches of Christ tend well over toward the left brain. We pride ourselves in being thinkers, not just feelers. But we need to remember that the gospel is partly right-brain. Not all of our left-brain tendencies came from the Bible. The roots of our Restoration Movement, which gave root to Churches of Christ, Christian Churches, and Disciples of Christ, ran deep into the left-brain intellectual soil of the nineteenth century, when the western world became "enlightened" and held high hopes for the power of reason. At least in part, the American dream grew out of this newfound confidence in the possibilities of the human intellect. This new country would avoid the social mistakes of less-enlightened societies.

Alexander Campbell, a key figure shaping the early stages of the American Restoration Movement, was a true son of the nineteenth century. When Campbell was a child, his father read him the writings of John Locke, one of the brain fathers of nineteenth-century rational enlightenment. Campbell later referred to Locke as "The Christian Philosopher." With apologies to Campbell and company, let me simply sketch out some of the resulting theological assumptions: Clear thinking would clean up the old religious muddle. God made the universe. Enlightened man could unlock the secrets of the universe. Therefore, since God also made man and the Bible, enlightened thinkers could unlock the mysteries of man and the Bible as well. Further, just as the new nation needed a constitution, so did the church. And the Bible was it.

Religious phenomena of the day influenced Campbell, too. One phenomenon was the subjective hyperemotionalism rampant in the frontier religion. For example, at Cane Ridge, Kentucky, in 1841, thousands gathered for a nineteenth-century religious "Woodstock." Mass psychology overwhelmed the crowd. Hundreds broke out in bizarre barking, jerking, and laughing which they attributed to outpourings of the Holy Spirit.

One can only imagine how all this clashed with Campbell's left-brained thought world. So Campbell pushed the Restoration pendulum toward the opposite extreme. Eventually, many restorationists limited the Holy Spirit to the status of retired author and limited worship to "five acts" stacked heavily on the left-brain side. Of course, the pendulum has begun to swing back some, but many, if not most, Church of Christ congregations may still be high-left.

In our honest attempts to keep the biblical foundations of our faith from evaporating into some amorphous better-felt-than-told experience, we in the Churches of Christ may not only have dwarfed our right brain but may have inadvertently screened a huge crowd out of our movement. Ironically, even as I am final-editing this book I received word that "right-brained Richard" (from our earlier discussion) has also left Old Paths Church and gone over to New Song Community Chapel.

OUR BOTH-BRAINED BIBLE

Besides screening right-brained people from left-brained churches, we may also have wrung the right-brain juices from our Bibles.

Aldous Huxley (author of *Brave New World)* speaks of man as a "multiple amphibian"; that is, we are designed to make our way through many worlds at once (intellectual, emotional, sexual, social, and so forth). But since the industrial revolution, we tend to live in the analytical sphere and crowd out those other worlds, which are thus atrophying, according to Huxley. Consequently, he believed, western mankind is losing touch with much of what it means to be human.

Something like this happens when faith zeroes in on the left-brain dimensions of Scripture (the informational, propositional, didactic) to the neglect of its right-brain elements. Our other worlds (the right-brain expanses of our nature) atrophy, and we may lose touch with much of what it means to believe. When we attempt to analyze and explain God, we may strip our faith of its drama, mystery, poetry, and story, which say about life and God what precept and reason can never say. Of course, faith is not irrational. Conversion brings a renewing of the mind and bids us *understand* what the will of the Lord is (Rom. 12:2). But on the other hand, we can never explain the inexplicable, ponder the imponderable, nor "unscrew the inscrutable." God is too vast and mysterious for that. So are human beings. There is far more to us than the cerebral side of our brains.

Scripture takes this into account and penetrates us on multiple levels, touching us at depths unreachable by information alone. Look, for example, at the variety of literary genre in Scripture. Some of the Bible is drama, some is music, some poetry, some narrative, some paradox and mystery. So the living Word can dance through all of our worlds, awakening them in ways too wonderful to explain.

However, our analytical roots bent the Church of Christ toward left-brain theology and left-brain styles of worship, which in turn attracted more left-brainers than right-brainers into our fellowship. Across several generations, we have evolved into what is by and large a full-blown left-brain religious culture.

RESIDENT ALIENS

Pat and Cheryl are telling us that some of our own children feel trapped in all this. After all, they didn't get to choose their roots, nor have they made a deliberate choice to be a part of our movement because they became attracted to it from the outside. They were born into it, even though God wired up some of them to be right-brained. They may be intellectually and culturally programmed to believe that left-brain theology and worship are somehow the right thing. Yet some feel emotionally alienated from their left-brain heritage, longing for something, even though they may not understand what it is. They may feel drawn toward some of the right-brain elements recently emerging in our worship and theology, but at the same time they are fearful. Some even register guilt over their own religious feelings. Others fear what cannot be analytically categorized!

Last Sunday, Toby, a single professional who recently began attending our congregation, stopped me and one of our elders in the aisle. Toby had just sung the lead solo in a moving contemporary Michael Card song, "In the Wilderness," during our worship. Most people usually find worship at our church to be very meaningful anyway, but last Sunday was one of those special days when the Spirit of God fell in rich measure on that place. Toby teared up and said, "When I first came here from my old church, I felt guilty for feeling the way I feel now at the end of a worship service. But now, I can't imagine honoring God any other way. Thank you! Thank you!"

Toby was a right-brained child reared in a left-brained church. What irony—when my God-given disposition collides with the very religious culture which taught me to love God!

Now, let's finish our conversation with Pat, the girl who collared me after class. Pat placed her fingertips to her temples, pondering as if to corner a slippery thought. Then she struggled on into her moment of truth.

"Actually, I don't want to deal with this. I can fill my 'feeler' needs in other places. And I have conditioned myself to 'get something' out of worship even though I don't like it much or don't feel much. I've given up a lot of myself to be faithful to the church. Why can't the rest?

"And Lynn, when you walk into class and lay that right-brain stuff beside the left-brain stuff, it stirs up both my longings and my fears. You set up an internal collision for me. I don't want to hear it. Why do we have to do these things? Why not just let sleeping dogs lie?"

Pat is one of those right-brained Christians reared in a left-brained church, and she's wrestling with convoluted feelings. At times, she feels drawn toward the freedom and expressiveness of right-brain worship, yet paradoxically longs for the security and orderliness of old familiar ways—feeling guilty when she enjoys an unfamiliar right-brain religious experience, yet feeling empty in the familiar left-brain worship service. Some right-brained Christians reared in left-brained churches resent their brothers and sisters who break loose and enjoy the emotional dimensions of faith, yet they secretly repress their own right-brain longings. Others may actually feel anger toward the left-brained churches for squelching their honest feelings. A most graphic example of this dilemma would be the nuns and the priest in the movie *Sister Act,* who both loved and feared the dimension of their natures being reawakened by the new worship style of the uninhibited character played by Whoopi Goldberg.

So what?

You may not be one of the right-brained Christians in a left-brained church. But nearly half of those raised in your congregation likely are. Does this mean that part of every church is doomed to be either frustrated or offended? Or that the congregation is destined to split? And what about right-brained Richard and his friends who steadily exit to other fellowships? I believe our times call for at least a three-fold response.

1. In all situations: Teach the whole word of God! Let our theology be both left- and right-brain—balanced as the Bible is.
2. In some situations: Renew, as the Lord gently, lovingly stretches the wineskins.
3. In other situations: Plant new congregations which begin with more balanced right- and left-brain styles.

Let me again traffic in hope! Fresh showers of blessings are riding on the winds of change!

Ideas are changing. For the last two decades, theology has moved steadily away from left-brain extremes. In my own fellowship, graduate Bible departments are strengthening our grip on the text and broadening our understanding of it as well. God is using pens in and out of my heritage like Rubel Shelly, Robert E. Webber, Jim Woodruff, Roland Allen, Leonard Allen, William Willomon, Richard Hughes, Gordon Borror, and others to help us rethink our theological foundations. And effective "street level" ministers are picking up on the right-brain hungers.

Style is changing, too. A resurgence of praise and worship is sweeping my fellowship as well as many others. We are beginning to see the Bible not so much as an anchor, but as a keel, and healthy fresh winds are blowing. God is using the pens of writers like Max Lucado (Wow! what a right-brainer!), Richard Foster, Henry Nouwen, and Calvin Miller to unpack our right brains, freeing us to feel our religion and releasing us to be "lost in wonder, love, and praise!" Through the talents of musically inclined men and women, God is leading us to include contemporary music and right-brain styles in our worship. But God is also reminding us that he is the audience and we are the participants. Worship is not meant to be experienced so much as to be offered, so that God might be glorified. May our lives and our worship make glad the heart of an awesome God who created us right and left.

> Take joy, my king,
> In what you hear.
> May it be a sweet, sweet
> Sound in your ear.[2]

Good days are ahead!

For many young people
in our churches and for
the non-churched visitor,
much of our music is a
foreign language.

CHAPTER NINE

MUSIC THAT MAKES SENSE

My two sons and I headed into the Rockies to conquer a few more "fourteeners" (that elite group of mountains peaking above 14,000 feet). The first morning, we drove off the highway up rock trails till we ran out of road, then hiked uphill for half a day and tented for the night. Next morning, we day-packed several hours up even steeper trails, climbing far above the timberline. Solitude at last! Deep in the wilderness, completely beyond the trash and gadgets of civilization.

But as we scrambled around a final switchback, we spied a lone figure on the summit. We shouted a greeting. No answer. Didn't notice us. Was he deaf? Then closer range solved the mystery. He was singing off-key and "bobbing to the beat," totally enwrapped in a world of music from his Walkman headphones!

Rock music? Deep in the wilderness? Why? Because he is part of a new culture that takes its "tunes" wherever it goes. Music is actually the most powerful language of the culture.

Music's appeal is not new, of course. Since the days of Jubal, "the father of all who play the harp and flute" (Gen. 4:21), we've loved it! But never before has music been the cultural force it has become in our times. In fact, each of us, individually, prefers some style of music that speaks to us, flows from our heart, which, if we had any musical talent at all, is the kind of music we would create. But just as that uniqueness of form varies from one person to another, so also it varies from culture to culture, from generation to generation, and certainly from one century to another.

SOUNDS FROM THE PAST

Music gets little notice in the early books of the Bible. Moses makes no mention of it. Amazingly, when God details Israel's tabernacle worship, music or singing isn't mentioned. Not until David designed the temple does Israel get instruction on music in worship. David organized choirs and trained musicians for the temple praise. But, prior to David's time, only sporadic outbreaks of song are noted: the song of Moses, Miriam's song of the women, Hannah's song of pregnancy. Apparently their music simply flowed from their hearts in their natural musical idiom.

Centuries later, the early church carried over the worship format from the Jewish synagogues, including music that would sound very strange today. Scripture readings were sung. But since there were no songbooks or standard musical score, the leader would sing a line of a psalm, improvising his tune. Then the congregation would respond, repeating the line and echoing the leader's tune. With standard psalms, the leader might sing the first verse, and the congregation respond with the second, and so on.

Everything, however, was improvisational. Not until relatively modern times was music written down and the form locked in place with a definite melody line and harmony. The chord structure and scale that we use today wasn't fully developed until the seventeenth century.

Back to the early Christians: As the church moved into Greek territory, the church quickly realized that Jewish sounds and melodies did not speak to the Greek heart. So, according to Clement of Alexandria, by A.D. 205 the church was adapting Greek music forms. These early forms would have sounded weird to modern ears. They kept every song within a total range of eight notes. For the happy songs, high pitched voices sang the top four notes. In sad songs, deep voices sang in a range of the bottom four. A strange sound, indeed. This Greek sound became the basis for the chants in the medieval church.

A second influence also shaped medieval church music. The Greeks worshiped multiple gods with drunkenness, licentiousness, and wild dancing to loud music. Christians said, "If our music sounds like their music, people may assume we do what they do." So, while church music was earlier built on Greek musical styles, later, the church intentionally created a sound that was distinctly different from the sound of pagan music. So, for several hundred years, common music and church music went separate ways.

BROTHER MARTIN'S CONTEMPORARY MUSIC

All that began to change in the middle ages. Around the tenth century, false teachers began effectively spreading heresy by putting it into popular songs. The church countered by setting orthodox teaching to popular tunes. But these were not for singing in public assemblies—only for private gatherings. As a result, beer-drinking songs and fun-loving songs in familiar melodies got dressed up in church garb.

Then, Martin Luther moved the "pop tune Christian music" into the public worship itself. This not only connected his message with the culture, but drew a contrast between the Reformation and traditional Catholicism. Thus, "new" music replaced the medieval chants.

By Luther's day, music inherited from the chants was sung in two parts with a tenor lead, which had been added around the twelfth century. Luther broke music out into four parts, but he soon realized that his people, being unschooled in music, couldn't learn the parts. So, Luther engaged a chorus of accomplished singers to stand up front and sing the parts, while the congregation sang the lead— thus began modern choirs, which became popular across the Protestant world. Luther's songs, besides opening the door for the rich Christian music that followed in Europe, also added his "new" theology of grace, spirit, and liberty via their lyrics. Interestingly, in Luther's day, "A Mighty Fortress Is Our God," which sounds ponderous to twentieth-century urban baby boomers, was the "new sound in contemporary music" and helped to usher in the new day of the Reformation.[1]

Notice the zigzag course across the centuries as Christian music repeatedly withdraws itself from the culture at one time, then reengages the culture at another. Strategies were carefully chosen in order to maintain Christian distinctiveness in one era and then to connect with the culture and enhance the effectiveness of Christian witness in another.

The zigzag of connecting–separating–reconnecting with the culture is nothing new. And music has been a powerful form across most of Christian history. But never before has music held anything like the overwhelming power that it holds in today's young urban world.

MUSIC: THE COIN OF THE REALM

Music wasn't always so ubiquitous, however. A hundred years ago, an occasional musician came through and filled a concert hall for a couple of hours. On special occasions, friends gathered around the fire to pick and sing. On Sundays they sang "church music."

Then sound recordings exploded on our ears. First came the old platter records. Then radio and TV, then tapes, then cassettes and CDs, until dens, automobiles, bedrooms, offices, and malls are flooded with music. Professional concerts not only fill civic centers, but thunder into our houses through TV. And now portable Walkman stereo sound follows us into the wilderness: omnipresent music, from all directions—powerful music, twenty-four hours per day! Today, music is indeed the coin of the realm.

Like it or not, we must realize that the most powerful influence in the lives of young people today is their music—more powerful than parents, than school, even than peers. If, in our culture, we do not communicate with the young through music, we simply do not communicate. Some of the strongest role models of the culture, for good or ill, are musicians. From Elvis to Madonna, music is power. No wonder someone said, "Let me write the songs of a nation and I care not who writes her laws."

A UNIVERSAL LANGUAGE?

Though music is universally appealing and the main heart language of our pluralistic culture, there is no singular music style that connects universally. In fact, various subcultures are set off from each other by their music, especially among youth. An adolescent can expect to be clearly "out" of a given group if he or she is "into" the wrong music. Depending on where you stand on the map, even the campus culture is splintered into a fast-moving kaleidoscope of segments: punkers, new-agers, head bangers, ropers, dopers, on ad infinitum. (If these categories were "in" when this chapter was typed, they will likely be "out" by the time you read it.)

Adult subcultures cluster around music, too. At the 1989 World Congress on Evangelism in Manila, Barbara King introduced me to the small but growing field of study called *ethno-musicology*. Ethno-musicologists count eight major distinct music groups on our planet. For example, even borderline tone-deaf listeners can detect a difference between sounds from Thailand, the drums of the Congo, the flutes of the Andes, and the bagpipes of Scotland. These major musical "continents" subdivide into countries and clans. Among our own Euro-American musical kinfolk, we find country music, rock, classical, mariachi, reggae, etc. Music may flourish universally, but it is inaccurate to describe music as a universal language.

In workshops, I frequently ask, "When you're driving down the freeway and flip on the radio, how many of you will likely select country western? Let me see a show of hands. How about rock? Easy listening? Acid rock? How many actually listen to a classical station?" I have run this poll all over the country and find that roughly 5 percent listen to classical music. Yet, have you noticed, in a lot of middle-of-the-road congregations, the classicals seem to plan the worship assemblies? No wonder many church-goers find "church music" boring and unrelated to life. And for the nonchurched visitor, much of our music is a foreign language.

Try planning a worship service in a church made of several subcultures spread across several generations. Each person wants to worship God in his or her own heart language, right? So, what songs will connect with them all? Usually, the entire congregation is subjected to the tastes of the minority who happen to be in control. This leaves the rest, even when they can't put their finger on the problem, scrambling to "translate" or else feeling emotionally left out!

And, if a sensitive leader chooses music to connect with the heart language of the fringe folks or the unchurched, then the "control" people get upset. The folks who don't connect with the music of the controlling group get upset too, but they don't usually demonstrate— they just disappear. They quietly vote with their feet. Folks with traditional music tastes may not even notice they have gone, much less understand why. If the most powerful language of the culture is music, even if we preach all the right words, yet still "speak in a foreign musical language," we will not connect with today's hearts. Rather, we will throw up barriers between our listeners and the gospel.

VANILLA MUSIC IN A BASKIN-ROBBINS WORLD!

To further complicate things, we have moved into a pluralistic culture. Back where I grew up, most people were first-generation western Europeans—same color, similar values, common lifestyle. Possibly it was like that for you in Muleshoe, Texas, or Sweet Lips, Tennessee, or Pumpkin Corner, Illinois. But not now—not by a long shot!

In a Baskin-Robbins urban world where five different languages can be heard between the parking garage and the office, the church must connect by speaking a variety of musical heart languages.

By musical languages, I mean two things: *idioms* and *formats*. Musical format is the way we present the music—either participatory (everyone participates or sings together) or presentational (the audience listens and the singers present). Variations of these two basic forms include congregational singing (everyone sings together), antiphonal singing (groups of the congregation sing back and forth to each other), choral music (a group sings to an audience), solos, and the list goes on.

On the other hand, musical idioms are forms and styles of music including such options as classical, traditional, Stamps-Baxter, country, rock, pop, etc. Make your own additions to the list. For our purposes here, idiom is the *type of music*. Format is the *style of presentation*.

A NEW SONG

In addition to the cultural reasons for a variety in idiom and format, there is also at least one "spiritual" reason. When we look through Scripture, new songs are frequently written to express expanding experiences with God. Example: "He put a new song in my mouth" (Ps. 40:3). New songs express new spiritual vistas. The old wineskins of the old songs may not stretch around the vintage of new spiritual growth. So, not only cultural variety, but spiritual growth calls for the creating of new and varied music.

NO-BRAINER MUSIC

In a research project conducted across the country, ABC radio discovered another need for new songs. ABC discovered that once a song is heard ten times, listeners no longer pay attention to its meaning. However, vain repetition—loss of meaning by overuse—is not to be confused with emphatic repetition—repetition for use of emphasis and emotional impact. A prime example of emphatic repetition is Psalm 136, in which the phrase "His love endures forever," is repeated twenty-six times. The Shema, recited at the beginning and end of every synagogue assembly, is another positive use of repetition. So, many contemporary praise and worship songs make this emphatic use of repetition. But, overuse of old songs can wash away the meaning.

Without variety, music that was once vibrant with meaning falls into meaningless repetition. With overfamiliarity, songs come in our ears and out our mouths without ever touching our hearts. This rote exercise actually trains congregations not to pay attention to the hymn's message. Ask yourself, how many times you have sung some of the old hymns. Even the excellent old hymns must often be recast in alternative arrangements or illustrated visually or sung with new emphasis to recover meaning afresh.

CONTEMPORARY MUSIC

To connect with today's heart language, we will need more contemporary music. Contemporary simply means "that which is common right now—current." Even so-called classical music was contemporary somewhere, sometime. Fanny Crosby's beloved hymns, "Blessed Assurance," "A Wonderful Savior," "To God Be the Glory," "Praise Him, Praise Him," "Tell Me the Story of Jesus," "Redeemed, How I Love to Proclaim It!" "I Am Thine, O Lord," "Jesus, Keep Me Near the Cross," "All the Way My Savior Leads Me," and "Rescue the Perishing," are traditional to us now. But they were contemporary about a hundred years ago. The music of Johann Sebastian Bach was contemporary in his day, although we now call it classical. Classical is a tag we attach to music that is good enough to have lasted a long time.

But because music is "good" music does not make it meaningful in the heart language of today. In order to communicate in the changing heart languages of the people, musical styles in worship must also keep changing.

What human communication factor in our assemblies could possibly be more important than music? Even shifting our preaching or educational strategies will not affect communication like choosing music that makes sense.

BASKIN-ROBBINS MUSIC IN THE BIBLE

Changing music in worship makes us nervous, however. Some churches hold long-standing and deeply entrenched traditions about acceptable and unacceptable music. But most of us are not afraid to go where the Bible takes us. So let's ask Scripture to diminish our fears.

One Sunday, a four-man worship team led our congregation in some new songs with words projected on screen. Since no sheet music was available, they sang the four parts using amplifying mikes, so each worshiper in the congregation could follow the part most comfortable to him or her. The song service that morning was mostly congregational singing; however, a trio sang to the congregation during the Lord's Supper. Their beautiful and poignant song set up our communion reflection. Afterward, a generous number of people affirmed, "Surely the Lord was in this place today!"

Later in the week, a card from an out-of-state visitor reached me, written in ball-point pen with such intensity that the ball-point broke through the card at some places. "Why do you do these things? Why four song leaders? Isn't one biblical enough? Why some people singing while others listen? Why not all sing together like the Bible says in Ephesians 5 and Colossians 3?" Possibly I should explain to the reader: In some camps among Church of Christ folk it is "unscriptural" to have choirs or singing groups (only congregational singing is acceptable), and one male song leader is our long-standing tradition.

I couldn't wait to check those texts to see if I'd missed something last time through! I opened to Ephesians 5:19 and found these words, "Speak to one another with psalms, hymns and spiritual songs. Sing and make music in your heart to the Lord." Guess what! I didn't find four song leaders in the passage. I didn't even find one song leader! Didn't even find an assembly! Only Christian hearts, filled with the spirit.

However I did find something interesting: several different musical idioms: psalms, hymns, and spiritual songs.

And I also found several different musical formats! "Speak to one another." My parents taught me it was rude to speak when someone else was speaking to me. "When we speak to one another," they coached, "we take turns." Ephesians 5 actually says that—at least some of the time—one group of people sings while another group listens. That can happen in several different formats: solos, trios, antiphonal singing, quartets, and a rich variety of other creative formats, in addition to everybody singing at once.

Then I flipped over to Colossians 3:16 to see what I had missed there. "Teach and admonish one another with all wisdom, and . . . sing psalms, hymns and spiritual songs with gratitude in your hearts to God." Combining Colossians with Ephesians, I found three purposes for music in worship. First I found *exaltation*—"to the Lord." In the largest and oldest songbook in print, 150 psalms are addressed "to the Lord." A significant but subtle shift in many worship assemblies recently has us singing more to God, not merely to each other about God. That is a big step in the right direction.

Second, I found *edification*—"teaching one another." It is very difficult to learn while we are talking. We must listen in order to learn. To teach via songs, some listen while others sing. Edify means to "build up." So besides teaching, singing may simply "build up" our spirits.

Third, I found *communication*—"speak to one another with songs." Thus, rather than forbidding singing groups in worship, Scripture actually enjoins them.

In 1 Corinthians 14:26, I found something else that I had not included in my old sermons on worship in assemblies: solos. (Again, in past times, some Churches of Christ considered church solos to be suspect.) "When you come together, each one has a hymn" (RSV) "or a word of instruction, a revelation, a tongue or an interpretation." "Speak, one at a time" (v. 27–NIV). If worshipers are to "speak, one at a time," with a tongue, interpretation, or prophecy, then when some Christian brings a song, he or she also should "speak" solo! Yes! biblical musical communication sometimes includes a solo, one person "speaking" in song to the rest of the congregation. Actually, in synagogue worship, and thus in the early church, solos were standard. When the Scripture was read publicly, it was actually sung.

So as it turned out, I'm thankful for my critical visitor's card. It drove me to discover that rather than commanding us to "all sing at one time," Scripture actually says exactly the opposite! Our fellowship could avoid much tension over music in the assembly if, instead of asking, "What am I comfortable with?" or "How did we do it last year?" we would simply ask, "What does the Bible say?" Biblical, scriptural worship is liberating, powerful, alive! After all, Church of Christ folks want to be a "people of the Book."

YES, BUT WHAT ABOUT . . . ?

Healthy change welcomes questions. Here are some questions I have heard in some Church of Christ subcultures concerning changes of musical format and idiom in worship:

➤ Isn't this faddishness?

After a century of congregational singing, must we now introduce singing groups just because others are doing so? Think about this: We started congregational singing because someone else was doing it! The pejorative word *faddish* can simply be a negative way of saying "current" or "in touch."

For example: how many worshipers drove to your church last Sunday in a 1950 automobile? I drove one in 1957, but I haven't owned one since. Today's cars are better, more appropriate for our times. Of course, serious churches do not simply want to jump on faddish bandwagons, but we must be authentic and effective. We must do business in the coin of the realm; that is, we must speak the musical heart language of the day. King James English doesn't fit normal communication nowadays. The language of the New International Version communicates better; and contemporary music fits better in most communities than classical or traditional. Fear of faddishness must not drive us to Amishness.

➤ Does not Scripture command all Christians to sing?

Of course. One great treasure of my heritage is congregational singing. I, for one, hope singing groups never replace congregational singing in my church. When congregational singing is vibrant and alive, some who hear it for the first time are enchanted. That is wonderful. But Scripture does not command all of us to sing at once! As we noticed in Scripture, congregational singing is augmented with presentations by soloists or singing groups.

➤ **If we use singing groups and solos in worship, is there not a danger they will become entertainment, rather than worship?**

Yes! And no! Jeff Nelson, our worship leader at Preston Road, insists steadfastly that no singing in worship must ever degenerate to the level of entertainment. Christians don't come to worship to be entertained. Jeff even flinches if a congregation applauds after a song. He fears the applause means, "Wasn't that a great performance?" (However, he is bending a little, since, in our culture, some applause is a way of saying "Amen.") Worship of God must not be mere entertainment.

But there is another way to look at this. The root word for *entertain* comes from the idea "to hold," as to hold someone's attention. At least in part, *entertaining* means interesting. Why do you prefer some Bible class teachers to others? Because they hold your attention, they are more interesting, right? In other words, they are more "entertaining" than the teachers who bore you to tears. Good teaching involves good communication. And good communication is partly entertainment. The same goes for preaching! We love the preacher who sometimes uses humor and who tells stories well. We listen to him better and learn more because he is, well, because he is entertaining!

One biblical purpose of singing is edification (teaching) and another is communication (speaking). Since good teaching and good communication involve elements of entertainment, good music will naturally be somewhat "entertaining."

"But," someone objects, "why must the singers stand up in the front and face the audience to sing?" Of course we *could* hide them, but *why?* Think this through: would you find your preacher's sermon as helpful and easy to follow if he were locked in a booth at the back while he preached and you merely listened to his voice over the sound system? No! You want to see him. While he speaks, he also communicates with his facial expressions, his gestures, his body language, even his clothing. Researchers tell us that communication is more than 90 percent nonverbal!

If not, we don't need any more preachers, lecturers, and Bible teachers. We just need more tapes! Tapes are cheaper and more mobile than preachers; plus, they can be duplicated. But if these nonverbal elements communicate during speaking *without* melody and harmony, they also communicate during speaking *with* melody and harmony. When singers stand in front of a congregation to minister in music, only a small part of the impact is the sound. They send constellations of supporting signals from their whole beings. These elements are lost if we hide the singers in the balcony and merely let their sound seep through. By the way, this is also one reason we carefully select worship leaders at our congregation. Jeff is far more concerned about the life and heart of leaders, than their gifts. But, of course, he also believes, as Scripture teaches, that they should be chosen by gift.

➣ Will not public displays of musical talents exalt persons and puff egos?

Yes, oh yes! And so will preaching, eldering, and song leading. Christians can even provide bedpan service in order to be thought humble and sincere. Most major blessings of God can be distorted. In fact the more spiritual the blessing, the more vulnerable to distortion.

In some honest moments, I must admit that one reason I step into the pulpit is that I love to stand in front of hundreds of people. "Wow! All these people came to listen to me speak. I must really be something!" One of the slipperiest spiritual struggles faced by public teachers of the Word is the conflict between that part of you that wants to be under the Lord and to help people, and that other part of you that wants to build a reputation, get attention, hold a job, or whatever motivates you. If you know how to clearly discern all of your motives, let me in on the secret. My phone number is 214-526-7221! Yes. There is danger. But we must not allow this fear to back us away from God's purposes for the power of music.

➣ Will not the congregation be passive, while only leaders express their worship?

If we only hear solos or singing groups, yes. Hundreds of churches across the country have become so dependent on a choir, a soloist, or instrumentation that their attempts at congregational singing are pitiful. Sure, that danger exists. Churches definitely don't want to lose our rich and precious tradition of congregational singing. And, by all means, we don't want to do anything that will develop passive pew-sitters. But, at crucial moments and occasions congregations can be powerfully engaged by musical presentations. Remember, God has given gifted musical communicators to the body. We don't want to waste those treasures.

➤ Will not these kinds of changes upset some people?

No question about that! The story of the people of God in Scripture is a story of repeated change, which usually disturbed some people. Why did some Israelites want to return to Egypt? Why was Paul stoned at Lystra? What was so disturbing about Stephen? Why was the book of Galatians written? And why the Jerusalem conference in Acts 15? And why did they crucify Jesus?

We must, of course, be very sensitive to beloved brothers and sisters who feel uncomfortable with change. I feel deeply troubled when would-be prophets march out and trample over the hearts of Christians who are not yet ready to move at the prophet's pace. This insensitivity reflects little genuine affection, little consideration of others above self (see Phil. 2:1-9). On the flip side, little growth or progress comes without painful stretching of wineskins! And longtime Christians or those uncomfortable with change are not licensed to consider their own interest over others either. This is also immature insensitivity.

You tell me. What should we do when young people are leaving us in droves because we are not connecting with their heart language and when hundreds of searchers check out our churches but don't come back because they don't understand the foreign language? Whose needs and feelings matter most to God? We must learn to navigate the white waters between the needs of the young and the searching on the one hand, and the feelings of those uncomfortable with change on the other. This is no small thing. If, as a Christian leader, I don't feel the pinch of this tension, either I may have become so entrenched that I will not change at any cost, or I may have become so wed to my own agenda that I run roughshod over people's feelings. Neither view is from God!

"WHAT I HEAR YOU SAYING IS . . ."

Let us summarize what we are *not* saying: As we call for new musical formats, we are not implying that these should replace congregational singing nor that a cappella churches should introduce instrumental music. And as we call for contemporary musical idioms, we are not suggesting that we jettison traditional hymns. Memory is a great treasure. Traditional hymns maintain ties with the past and preserve faith history.

Let us also summarize what we *are* saying:

➤ **We are calling for some new ways of using music in worship to connect with the new and varied heart languages of our culture.**

Both at the Highland Church of Christ, where I ministered twenty years, and now at Preston Road, where I have been for two years, we circulated questionnaires surveying the congregation's tastes in musical styles and formats. We formed grids listing cultural groups across the top and age groups down the side, thus mapping tastes and comfort zones. Worship-planning sessions ask, "Who did we leave out last week?" Or, "What musical format and idiom will connect with this group or that?" In this way we are attempting to assure that no one heart language gets either neglect, on the one hand, or undue attention, on the other. Frequently, we also publicly explain, with a statement something like, "This is a church of variety, but also of deep mutual respect and love. In that spirit, today we are celebrating the heart language of those who like X; next week we'll be celebrating the heart language of Y."

➤ At times, special music can do what congregational singing cannot do.

One Sunday morning, the special communion trio I mentioned earlier, sang "Create in Me a Clean Heart, Oh God." The congregation did not know that particular song, so by singing it to us, the trio helped us express emotions for which the congregation knew no song. Their song exactly fit the mood of repentance and confession conveyed in that communion moment. The congregation sat profoundly moved and with uplifted faces as tears flowed. A gifted musician can also minister encouragement, teaching, and instruction, even with the use of familiar, traditional music.

➤ Singing groups can connect with a culture who are watchers and listeners, but not participators.

The average person who comes in from the world as a guest on our pews, as well as persons from today's churched "CD culture," are used to being sung to; thus, presentational music communicates to them.

➤ Variety in musical idioms and formats enters people's hearts through many different doors.

Congregational singing is one beautiful and powerful means of expression; so is classical music. Contemporary music is another. Presentations of special music is yet another. A variety of heart doors beckon from our pluralistic and rapidly changing culture.

➤ **A variety of musical idioms and formats connects with a wider variety of people in our culture.**

Do you ever wonder how many people in your own church are hanging in only because they have learned to survive your tastes? Out of loving concern for them, why not move outside your tastes and comfort zones? In so doing, you may also connect with a wider circle of unchurched seekers.

➤ **Music that makes sense will harness the power of contemporary music for the Lord.**

Why let the devil have it all? The central reason for variety of musical idiom and format in worship is because the Bible calls for it!

Some Christian friends near my home in the Dallas/Fort Worth Metroplex invited their unchurched next door neighbor to visit church with them. She loved them, so she accepted. Monday afternoon, over the back fence, they eagerly fished for her impressions. "It was nice," she said.

"Nice?"

"Well, you won't be offended if I get honest? Where in the world did you get that weird music?"

Could that have been your church or mine?

The howling winds of change are filling our ears and our churches with the sounds of new music!

THE ART OF CHANGE MANAGEMENT

"The harder I push, the harder the system pushes back."

Peter Senge[1]

The change agent must maintain a delicate balance between being a strong pioneer leader and an integrated group member.

MINIMIZING CHAOS

The Scottish poet, Robert Burns, penned these lines:

> The best laid schemes o' mice and men
> Go oft awry
> And leave us naught but grief and pain
> For promised joy.[2]

Now, if you don't believe Burns, ask Uzzah! Or Edsel Ford or Saddam Hussein or the last guy who decided he was going to make all those fancy changes in his church!

We have now arrived at the climactic section of this book: *The Art of Change Management.* Concepts in this and the next four chapters may be new to many of our readers; but understanding them is well worth the effort required, because they will put in your hands some of the most basic tools for navigating the winds of change that are howling at your church door.

As this section title indicates, change management is more nearly an art than it is a science. Art does not follow formulas and rigid rules, rather it is a *creative* process; and the art of change management is also a *cooperative* process. Even so, definitive skills are needed if we are to navigate change "artfully."

While the term *management* is a useful one (and is used in this section title), perhaps an even more appropriate term is *navigation*. It is crucial that we do not begin with a commonly held (but very wrong) idea that the role of the change agent is to manipulate others and force his or her changes upon them. Neither is his or her role one of an "infallible" leader who arbitrarily sets policy for a group of which he is not an integral part. Rather, the change agent must maintain a delicate balance between being a strong pioneer leader and an integrated group member.

In some ways, the change agent is like the Old West wagon master, who lead wagon trains stretching far behind him and over the horizon across the treacherous West toward California. The wagon master knew that if he went too fast, the young, the old, and the sick would not be able to keep up. But he also knew that if he went as slowly as this group *wanted* to go, they may all die when winter set in. Since there was no turning back, his job was to get them through the mountains before winter —even though the required pace could cause some precious people to be lost along the way. So he traveled as slowly as he could in order to bring the strugglers along,

but not so slowly that they would fail to reach their destination before winter. This is the challenge of the change
agents facing the chill winds of change in our times. They
must be sensitive to the needs of those who find change
overwhelming, but they must not move so slowly that the
whole church perishes.[3]

So as we use the terms *change management* or *change
manager,* understand that we do not mean to imply that a
leader is a manipulator. In actual fact, no one can
"change" people or "manage" change. Perhaps the term
change navigator better describes the role. It suits the
premise, not merely the title, of this book.

The chill winds of change are blowing across the culture and the church with irresistible velocity; and change,
by its very nature, wreaks some level of chaos. While I do
not pose as an expert change "artist," I do offer some principles that can help you manage, or navigate change, instead of letting it manage you, and that can help you
minimize the ensuing chaos. The concepts of this chapter
come from several resources and have been combined
with my own experience across thirty-five years of scrambling to keep up with changing times.

UNDERSTAND THE INFLAMMATORY NATURE OF CHANGE

The first rule in minimizing chaos: Never underesti-
mate the inflammatory nature of even the word *change.*

Dr. Fred Craddock of Emory University tells this story:
While on an out-of-town speaking engagement, Craddock
was invited to dinner at the home of a middle-aged couple. Both host and hostess were divorced from previous

mates and had been married to each other only a few weeks. Dr. Craddock was their first dinner guest.

"We sat down to an elegant table," recalls Craddock, "White linen. Stem crystal. Fine china. And the heaviest, most ornate silverware I've seen." Since the host couple was nervous and Craddock was a stranger, conversation began awkwardly. Fumbling for words to fend off the ominous silence, the hostess picked up her ornate fork, examined it from several angles and commented, "You know, I don't like this fork!"

With that, her husband stood, abruptly threw his balled-up napkin in his plate and slid his chair against the table with enough force to rock water from the glasses. Then he turned on his heel and left Dr. Craddock and the mortified woman alone with the fallout.

"Being a man of the cloth," Craddock said, "I felt I should say something, so I ventured, 'I don't think those forks are all that bad!'" Craddock's comment triggered her tears, "Boo hoo. I don't know why I said that," she wailed. "All he brought to this house when we married was this silverware. When his first wife threw him out, her parting words were, 'and you can take your mother's [expletive deleted] silverware with you!'"

Craddock reflects painfully, "It never would have occurred to me that an innocent little word like *fork* could carry so much explosive baggage."4

In that setting, the innocent word *fork* carried ominous overtones. The word *change* can be even more explosive, especially in church circles. And, like the word *fire,* it is rarely neutral. If you tell me there is a warm fire crackling on my hearth, that's wonderful. But fire running up my living room drapes is entirely another matter! Change, too, can be very wonderful or very terrible.

CONSIDER *WHAT,* *WHY,* AND *HOW* TO CHANGE

We make no attempt to fully answer these three huge questions right here. But we must carefully consider each of these factors before jumping headlong into change. You may want to go back and review previous sections of this book where, *what* and *why* are explored. You may also want to gather a circle of godly peers in your congregation and pray over these questions.

First, consider *what* to change. Remember: some things definitely *must not be changed!* We dare not tamper with eternal foundations. These are the same in Botswana as they are in Boston; they are the same in the first century as in the twenty-first. These absolutes remain "the same yesterday and today and forever" (Heb. 13:8). Of course, not all change is good. However, as we have insisted in previous chapters, some things *must change—* and keep on changing as the culture changes.

Next, consider *why* a certain change is being proposed. While it is true that in many instances we must change or fail, change merely for change's sake rarely helps a church. Let's review some legitimate reasons to change things in a church:

- To encourage authentic and free worship in the heart language of today's people.
- To connect with the unchurched world for outreach and effective assimilation of new Christians into the body.

- To intentionally nurture spiritual life development in the people God sends our way.
- To do everything with the excellence that honors and glorifies God.
- To be faithful to God. God never changes, but he has designed his church so that it can continually reshape to connect with all cultures of an ever-changing world. Even in New Testament days, the churches show a different "look" from one city to the next as the gospel crossed cultural barriers.

However, knowing what to change and why is only part of the equation. Knowing *how* to change is equally crucial. Thus, in these days of transition, the most important tools for church leaders may be skills in the art of change management. As Lyle Schaller puts it,

> After more than three decades spent working with thousands of congregational, denominational, seminary, and para-church leaders from more than five dozen traditions, this observer places a one-sentence issue at the top of that list: The need to initiate and implement planned change from within an organization . . . reversing a period of numerical decline requires changes. Numerical growth also produces change. That means the key to the effective implementation of a church growth strategy is skill as an agent of planned change. . . . It may mean a change in the criteria for recruiting and training a new generation of leaders."[5]

Thank you, Lyle. My corner of the room erupts with a rousing, "Amen!" Unfortunately, most congregations have a few people with enough clout to cause serious disruption but not enough discipline and maturity to become informed on the skills of effective change management.

I found this out the hard way!

PROCEED WITH CAUTION

In August of 1992, Jeff Nelson and I led a conference in Dallas called *A Church that Connects.* We were stunned at the level of interest. We expected less than 150 participants, but more than 600 people showed up from more than 200 congregations from 19 states. Similar interest continued when we repeated the seminar at the Pepperdine University Lectureship in Malibu, California, and at five other metropolitan centers. In this seminar, we explored key changes needed in today's urban congregations. People got fired up; they charged out of the seminar and hit their home congregations broadside with the most out-on-the-edge new things they had heard at *Connects I.*

Consequently we have been getting phone calls all year. Some good people inadvertently contributed more to problems than to solutions. In fact, one or two ministers may be seeking new employment by now! Many good intentions backfired because of naiveté about the complexity of managing change; and I believe we may have inadvertantly set some of them up for trouble. Thus, our 1993 *A Church that Connects II* seminar was distinctly different from the *Connects I.* Rather than headlining our 1992 theme of the *need* for change (which included the why and what to change), in 1993 we majored on theory and skills for the art of change agency—*how* to change!

Change is not an option. It is a given. Change happens! But understanding the inflammatory nature of change, we must proceed with caution. These next few chapters summarize the gist of the 1993 seminar and provide insights on *how* to change.

KNOW YOUR LIMITS

Another step in minimizing chaos for would-be change agents is to know your limitations. There are some things that leaders/change agents definitely cannot do. For example:

➤ You cannot change a person's tolerance for change.

This tolerance is inherent to each person's unique makeup. Some simply like change better than others. (See Figure 1 later in this chapter.)

➤ You cannot force people to change.

This is related to the what-we-really-need-here-is-a-bigger-hammer syndrome. We become ecclesiastical versions of *Home Improvements'* Tim the Tool-man Taylor, who seems to think every problem can be solved by increasing the voltage. But this strategy only causes the system to lock up or to break. As Peter Senge says, "The harder I push, the harder the system pushes back." Temporary compliance can be forced, but the resulting compliance is rarely positive in the long run.

➤ You cannot form people's perceptions for them.

The totality of past experience and current situation shapes how one will perceive a change. This makes perception personal, unique, and sometimes change-resistant. You can help people *examine* their percpetions (as we will discuss later), but you cannot *form* perceptions for another person.

CIRCUMVENT FAILURE

Overzealous and underinformed change agents often meet with strong resistance, but the wise change navigator can circumvent unnecessary opposition and minimize chaos by following the principles outlined below:

➤ Don't try to copy the strategies of others.

Some try to copycat "effective" churches like Saddleback Valley Community Church, outside Los Angeles, or the Willow Creek Community Church, near Chicago, which are growing at phenomenal rates. We can (in fact, we ought to) learn a great deal from effective community churches, but copycatting is dangerous. There is a crucial difference between a principle and a method (or strategy). While basic growth principles may be transferable to any community, the specific methods and strategies used to apply these principles in one setting will seldom transfer to another.

For example: *Principle*—Outreach events must be expressed in the musical heart language of your culture. *Application*—In Chicago or Los Angeles, a contemporary "pop" musical idiom may connect. But is that the right musical idiom for Fort Worth, Texas, or Lepanto, Arkansas, or Nashville, or Watts? Effective churches extensively research their communities. They know exactly who their target group is and have tailored their strategies for *their* target people, not for the folks in *your* community. It may be helpful to apply *principles* from effective churches, but it is dangerous to copy their *strategies.*

➤ Carefully evaluate your motive for change.

Inexperienced change agents sometimes operate from skewed motives: "I like this better," or sometimes even, "Let's show those other folks who is in charge." Quite often, the "changer" would shift things around to his or her own liking, rather than considering the likings of the people that his or her church should be trying to serve.

➤ Examine your change implementation approach.

Some wrong approaches of implementing change include: heavy-handedness, manipulation, "executive decision," or the wing-it-till-they-whack-us style.

➤ Change things at an appropriate pace.

William Bridges, who wrote *Managing Transitions,* says that "the real problem is not in bringing about change, but to keep too much change from happening too fast."[6] The attitude of many seems to be: "If next year would help, *immediately* will cure everything." Sometimes the urgency of the convinced ignores the feelings of the unconvinced. This is both unloving and counterproductive.

➤ Do not introduce the most important changes at the point of greatest risk.

The most important changes should not be introduced at the point of greatest risk—the Sunday morning assembly. Important changes must be introduced with care—perhaps at a retreat or on Wednesday or Sunday nights. In the minds of many, Sunday morning assemblies are the most "sacred" time and the most sensitive place and thus should be least tampered with. Be wise and thoughtful in your introduction of change.

UNDERSTAND TEMPERAMENT DIFFERENCES

Minimizing chaos is also expedited when we understand the differences in how people respond to change. While a congregation as a whole may stand at a specific stage on the transition continuum, individual persons within that system will fall all over the map. The following bell curve helps us understand why. Part of the differences in how people handle change, is a matter of temperaments. Everett Rogers, in *Communication of Innovations,* sees five levels of change tolerance.

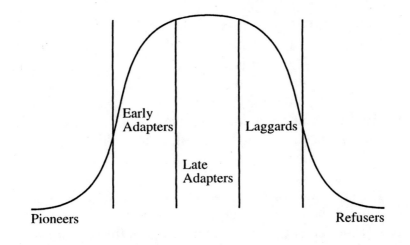

Figure 1. **Levels of Change Tolerance**
Adapted from Everett M. Rogers with F. Floyd Shoemaker[7]

With changing issues and life circumstances, each of us may show differing styles. On some issues we may be laggards or refusers, and on others, we may be pioneers, but our basic temperaments hold true most of the time.

➤ Pioneers

Approximately 8-10 percent of the people in most congregations will be pioneers (of whom yours truly is one). Pioneers are eager to explore new territory and launch into new experiments. They are the Christopher Columbuses of the congregation, ready to sail off the map.

➤ Early Adapters

These people are not going to be the first to move out. But, they will likely be right behind the pioneers and the first ones to support them. Usually, they are opinion leaders. Opinion leaders don't wait around to see what everyone else thinks before they move out.

The Restoration Movement appears to have been launched by pioneers and early adapters. Campbell and Stone broke new trail and seemed undaunted by the price they paid and unafraid of where their direction might lead them. To talk about a conservative restoration movement is an oxymoron. When you stop and think about it, restorationism is a radical idea that gave rise to a radical movement.

Recently, one of my respected friends suggested that to safeguard the unity of our brotherhood and the solidarity of our movement, we should avoid both the radical "left" and the radical "right" and should rather seek to be radical "centrists." While I appreciate the intent of that statement, I could not disagree with it more. Radical centrist is a political position, not a theological one. And it is completely at odds with the highest ideals of the Restoration Movement, which calls people to be accountable to Christ alone, through Scripture alone. From day one it has warned against the dangers of allowing one's denominational affiliation to shape one's convictions or practices. I would plead with us not to lose that pioneering spirit and to be *radically biblical,* as best we understand what that means. This will not always put us at the center. At times this will look leftist, as it did on race relations during the sixties. At other times it will look rightist, as it does now on abortion and homosexuality. Any other road to unity leads away from the ideals of our movement, toward the disintegration of our personal integrity, and into a sectarian denominational mindset.

➤ Late Adapters

Late adapters will support change all right, but not until the early adapters do, especially the early adapters they consider to be opinion leaders. Most congregations are made up primarily of people in this temperament group. In other words, rarely are the majority of people in a congregation pioneers or even early adapters, except possibly in a new church plant. A wise change agent will wait for this group's acceptance before he proceeds with a mega-move. This might mean giving the church at least six months adaptation time before a major innovation is adopted.

➤ Laggards

Laggards are not going to change until the new way has become the norm or the majority position. Laggards are uncomfortable being in an abnormal or minority position. Group identity is their comfort. But when it appears inevitable that everybody is eventually going to do it the new way, they will follow along and become enthusiastic supporters of accepted changes—that is, as enthusiastic as laggards get about anything!

The three groups in the middle—early adapters, late adapters, and laggards—likely make up about 80 percent of the average congregation or organization.

➤ Refusers

Finally, at the extreme right end of the bell curve are the refusers. This group constitutes the 8–10 percent of an organization that are not likely to change, no matter what.

Warning: These five types are not gradations of character quality, nor is one group more or less spiritual than the other. They are simply wired up differently, and individuals of each temperament type must be respected for who they are. However, it should be understood that people can also fall into one of these five categories on the basis of their conviction or values, not necessarily by predisposition. Some are honestly anchored to their niche on the bell curve by their beliefs and cannot make a particular change as a matter of conscience.

Whether by conscience or by temperament, in most churches, almost 8 percent are in the "wrong church." The trouble is, they may not have any options, especially if their church is the only game in town.

RECOGNIZE TENDENCIES OF VARIOUS GROUPS

While understanding the danger inherent in labeling one another, the following chart and list, from the Fuller

Evangelistic Accociation, offer valuable insight into ourselves and others. Don't use this chart to label your fellow
Christians, but apply it wisely and lovingly as you navigate
through change.

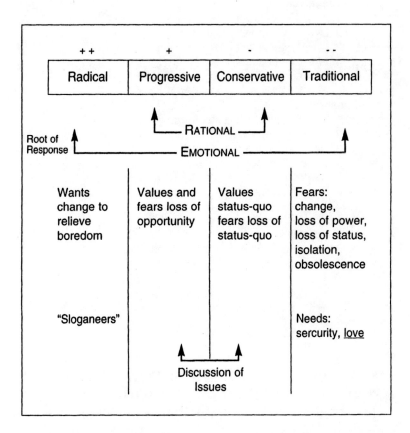

Radicals
1. Source of many good ideas
2. Provide "leavening in the dough mix"
3. Not a good source of input to leadership
4. Early starters—quick burnout

Progressives
1. Tuned to anticipate youth needs
2. Live on the growth edge
3. Quickly perceive benefits in good planning
4. Will spearhead new directions
5. Best communicators to conservatives
6. Risk takers

Conservatives
1. See the value of the status quo
2. Do not generally jeopardize personal comfort
3. Need real answers to real questions
4. Will keep leadership honest
5. Carry most of the financial burden
6. Not risk takers

Traditionalists
1. Extremely resistant to change
2. Operate in an emotional climate
3. Do not support change of any kind
4. Never buy in

Figure 2. **Typology of Change Respondents**
©1982, Fuller Evangelistic Association

DECIPHER THE DIFFERENCE BETWEEN HONEST DISSENT AND DYSFUNCTION

In addition to temperaments and convictions, another significant factor comes into play. As Kenneth Haught points out in his excellent book, *Antagonists in the Church,* a given percentage of the people in any organizational culture are dysfunctional. Most enterprises (business, educational, and the like) know what to do with dysfunctional people. They do not *reward* them; there-

fore, they do not *empower* them. They may not fire them.
They may send them for treatment or move them to an in-
nocuous job in the mailroom. But they do not reward
them for dysfunctioning all over a healthy organization.

However, in the church, out of misuse of such phrases
as "weaker brother," "causing stumbling," or even
"priesthood of believers," we frequently treat dysfunctional people as if they were responsible players. And
when they dysfunction on us (especially on the elders,
who are often already drowning in the demands of dysfunctional people), we reward them for that dysfunction
by giving in to them or by treating them as if they had a
normal contribution to make to the system. By rewarding
them, we empower them and allow them to take the
church hostage. We see it happening all over the country.
Many churches are actually being steered by the dissent-
ing vote or the squeaky wheels, which all too often are
made up of dysfunctional people. Not only is this a misuse of Scripture and a travesty of the concept of the priesthood of believers, but it is unloving to treat a
dysfunctional person as if he or she were functional. And
it is damaging to the church!

Please don't hear me suggesting that every refuser is
dysfunctional. Of course, it would be simple enough to
believe that people who disagree with me are dysfunctional. No, I am certainly not implying that people who
are slow to adapt to change by disposition, conviction, or
lack of information are dysfunctional. But there are genuinely dysfunctional persons in most churches, as in any
other organization. And when dysfunctional persons are
allowed to change the shape of a system, the system itself
becomes dysfunctional. Ken Haught's book is written
partly to help identify dysfunctional people and to clearly

differentiate them from responsible dissenters. Haught also articulates loving, responsible ways to minister to dysfunctional people while at the same time going on with the mission of the church.

If you are convinced that dysfunction is being rewarded in your church, one constructive thing you can do is suggest Haught's book as a diplomatic way to help your shepherds understand the dysfunction.

Change agents who are themselves open to change, who welcome evaluation of their ideas, and who listen to others, will enable people to move toward the innovative end of the bell curve—to enable laggards to move toward becoming pioneers or at least early adapters. However, there will always be a small group of refusers, and the God-given mission of your church cannot wait on their good will. In fact, to allow this not only stalls the church, but also spins the pioneers and early adapters out of your church and attracts more refusers, making needed change less likely with each passing year.

Rewarding the initiatives of pioneers and early adapters, on the other hand, creates momentum in your church. It attracts positive, energetic people and fosters a visionary, optimistic spirit. And the more these people are attracted to your church, the more flexible, adaptable, and effective it will become. It will become capable of refining and upscaling its models and methods so that your church can:

- reach an ever-changing culture
- nurture the growth of believers
- hold the loyalty of our oncoming generation
- worship more vibrantly and authentically in the heart language of the culture
- glorify God and pursue his mission

While some chaos cannot be entirely avoided as we face the chill winds of change, the chaos can be significantly minimized. Thoughtful change agents will not ignore sound change principles as they carefully, "artistically" navigate the winds of change.

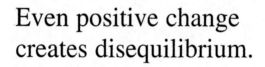

Even positive change
creates disequilibrium.

CHAPTER ELEVEN

GETTING CHANGE INTO YOUR SYSTEM

ORGANIZATIONAL CHANGE

To change a church is to change a *system*. Companies such as EDS and American Express, realizing the complexity of changing systems, are developing teams of skilled change agents. Carey Garrett, a sister in our congregation and coauthor of much of this section is one of those who helps companies undergoing radical transformation. Think about this: If fast-moving, successful corporate giants have difficulty in changing rapidly enough to stay in touch, how much more intentionality is needed to keep old, slow-paced, traditional organizations like churches in touch with the times.

161

➤ The "Systems" Approach

A good deal of what we know about the art of change management grows out of the "systems" approach in current marriage and family therapy. The systems school holds that a family is not merely a collection of individuals, but an intertwined organism. Significant change in any one member of a family, even when that change is positive, usually disturbs the ecology of that family; consequently, a psychotic person treated solo may show remarkable recovery—until he or she goes back home. Then, in a few weeks, the progress made in therapy usually comes unraveled because the individual returns to a troubled family *system*—which automatically presses that individual back into the behavior that fits his or her role in the family.

My friend, Dr. Royce Money, often says, "a church is more like a family, than anything else." I agree. So, when we talk about changing a church, we are not dealing with a mere collection of independent units, but an organism; an extended family system. And a church is infinitely more complex than a nuclear family unit.

Rabbi Edwin Friedmann, in 1986, was among the first to apply the systems theory to church and synagogue life in his must-read and still current book, *Generation to Generation.*[1] Many since Friedmann have applied the systems theory to all types of organizations. Among these is Peter Senge who wrote *The Fifth Discipline,* in which he calls the flexible, healthy organizational system a "learning organization"—not in the sense that it gathers information, but in that it is constantly adapting its structure, management style, strategy, and so on. I believe Jesus designed the church to be such a learning organization, so that it can flex to connect with any cultural setting.

➤ Laws of Organizational Change

Senge thumbnails the complexity of changing a "system" in his "Laws of Organizational Change":[2]

Today's problems come from yesterday's solutions.

For example, twenty new babies a year for the last two years called for expanded nursery space at our church. Yesterday's solution: the nursery took over Adults #2's classroom. Today's problem: Adults #2 Class (made up mostly of parents of nursery children) was left without a room. Yesterday's solution—the nursery—became today's problem for the adult class.

The harder you push, the harder the system pushes back.

For those who have tried to push a change in your congregation, no elaboration is needed on this point.

Behavior grows better before it grows worse.

People may appear to go along with a change, at first, but just wait!

The easy way out usually leads back in.

Watch for the "gotcha!"

The cure can be worse than the disease.

Research indicates that some 50 percent of changes introduced into businesses will be toxic to those businesses in the future. I'd guess that goes for churches too.

Faster is slower.

Remember: An attempt to move a church from a one to a ten in a single fell swoop may crystallize at a point far below zero.

Cause and effect usually are not closely related in time and space.

Physically, this happened to Dizzy Dean when his compensation for a broken toe shifted his form just enough to torque his arm and eventually destroy his professional baseball career. In a church it may go like this: add needed staff now by borrowing money, which may be fine for two years. Then the resulting growth calls for building expansion, which costs money. But the money won't go around, and you already owe the bank.

You can have your cake and eat it too, but not all at once.

We may be able to have both innovative, contemporary worship styles, and the financial support of traditionally thinking members, but usually not all at once. However, given time and wise change strategies, we may have both.

Now, here's my favorite . . .

Dividing an elephant in half does not produce two small elephants.

A doctor doesn't keep your sore arm at his office for treatment and tell you to pick it up next week after he works on it a while. It is part of a system. Nor can we fix a church by pulling a piece aside and tinkering with it as if it were an autonomous unit. No, a church too is an organism, an integrated system.

HOW CHANGE WON'T GET INTO YOUR SYSTEM

Before learning Peter Senge's "Laws of Organizational Change," I had worked out a few principles from my own experience on how change won't come into your system.

➣ Change will not come until a group sees the need to change.

In other words, change won't happen in churches until the status quo is intolerable. Why would people want needless change? Why disturb a peaceful church?

Herein lies the reason I have so bluntly asserted that many churches in our fellowship must change or die! It's also the reason we spent early chapters on bad news and shattered dreams. I believe the status quo *is* intolerable. Most of our congregations have plateaued or are in decline. Fewer than 5 percent are growing by evangelism, although many are "swelling" via transferring members. Dedicated and bright young people leave us in throngs and head down the street to churches that speak their language. This is intolerable!

I love our fellowship and have no plans to leave. True, we have a lot to learn. But we *do* have something unique and precious to offer. So for me, it is intolerable to stand by and watch antiquated formats and ineffective strategies drag our fellowship down the drain.

Let's refuse to throw in the towel. Sure, some folks will not change even when they see the handwriting on the wall. However, most Christians, once they catch a vision of what God can do through us if we reconnect with our culture, will run toward the needed changes. So good change agents must clearly and constantly help people understand (1) the value of changes, (2) the biblical ratio-

nale for changes, (3) the parameters of changes being proposed, and (4) how change preserves what has always
been of ultimate importance: the cause of Jesus Christ.

➤ Change will not come without resistance.

Most new change agents assume that everyone will automatically go for changes that will obviously improve
effectiveness. Wrong! When resistance surfaces, green
change agents tend to assume the proposed change must
be wrong, and they back off. But resistance doesn't necessarily mean your proposed change is wrong. On the
contrary, resistance is a normal part of change.

Ronnie White, from the Quail Springs Church of
Christ in Oklahoma City, says, "Most 'changers' don't
appreciate the pain involved in change. If you change too
fast some people leave. If you change too slow, others
leave. Either way, it hurts."

Ronnie is right! Change produces a grief separation
from past comfort zones, memories, and traditions. Even
if I don't like what I have been doing and I am going to
like what comes, I still feel a sense of loss—loss of comfortable habits, precious traditions, and close relationships I have formed. Change takes these from me and
replaces them with new things or new ways of doing
things.

Carey Garrett, my friend who works professionally in
change management, explains that resistance to change
usually evolves through four distinct stages.

Denial

Resistance usually begins slowly with a refusal to ac-
knowledge that the change is really happening. People in

denial do nothing. The memo comes down that your company has reorganized and there is a new way that you fit into the picture. But it may take a few months for people to really understand what is going on. During that time, there may be no loss in productivity; things may even get better.

This also happens when preachers or elders suddenly get up one Sunday morning and announce some sweeping change. At first the congregation thinks the leaders don't really mean it. Or, they believe that if they drag their feet long enough, it isn't going to happen. But, when it does happen and keeps on happening, the congregation gets mad or scared and resistance begins.

Resistance

After denial, comes resistance proper; people become abruptly aware of the changes and begin truly resisting. They become painfully aware of the significance of the change and the personal implications for them! With the onset of this stage, the organization or church loses its momentum and productivity plunges. The once unified team no longer keeps its eye on the goal. Folks become concerned about the "me" issues. How will this affect me? How does this change alter my role here? What impact will it have on my relationships with others. These concerns drain organizational energy. In a church, this stage may mean attrition in volunteer ministry, a drop in the number of conversions, declining attendance, or free-falling giving levels.

Remember, these stages won't always be obvious. Daryl Conner, in his book *Managing at the Speed of Change,* points out that resistance surfaces in two ways—

overtly and covertly.³ When people overtly resist, they may demonstrate anger, doubt the change, and argue why it will not work. When people covertly resist, they may go underground, undermine efforts to change, or just become very complacent, exhibiting passive-aggressive resistance.

Overt resistance, although more uncomfortable and potentially confrontational, is always preferable to covert resistance. Overt resistance is honest and open. It's no fun, but at least you know where it's coming from. Covert resistance is inward and quiet and is often difficult to spot, especially at first. Sometimes, "inward" people even get physically sick during change. Covert resistance is hard to identify and therefore hard to deal with and work through.

What is risky about the resistance stage is that some people can "check out"; that is, physically leave the job or the congregation or the fellowship. This is devastating! Probably even more damaging, however, is when people *physically* stay around the church but *mentally* check out. One example of this is when covert resisters simply withhold their financial offerings as a form of passive aggression.

Exploration

Regaining momentum after stage two is often no easy task, but if a system is skillfully piloted through the wild turbulence of resistance, it can emerge into a third stage: exploration.

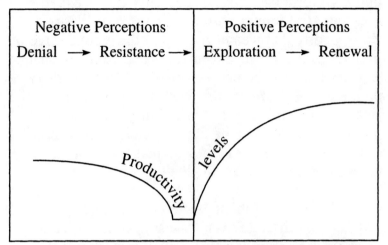

Figure 3. **Human Responses to Change and Productivity Levels**
Combined and adapted from charts by Joe Beam and Carey Garrett

Until now, people will have held negative perceptions of the change (toward the left side of the graphic). But in the exploration phase, their perceptions of change will shift toward the positive (toward the right side of the graph). This is when people see light at the end of their tunnel—positive possibilities for themselves and for the congregation. At this point, production levels begin to climb upward.

During exploration, people need direction and a vision of what the future will look like! They also need to know their roles in the change.

Renewal

The final stage is renewal. In this stage people begin to commit and energize. Things may still be ambiguous to them, but by now they are more comfortable with the ambiguity. Unfortunately, some churches never experience stages three and four because the first two stages are managed so poorly that we never get past the second stage. A big factor in this mismanagement is that so many change agents try to hurry the process and do not allow *adequate time for internal adjustment.* The most common mistake of inept change management is to hurry the process.

Of course, the goal of church leadership is healthy progress through these stages of personal change. This takes a lot of time and (again, don't forget this) usually includes a calculated dip in growth or productivity or changed lives during the transition (see Figure 3).

We all pass through every one of the stages, although people progress through them at different speeds. If a change is introduced to four people at the same time, some weeks later, one may be in denial, another in resistance, another in exploration, and one might have already reached renewal. This is because each person responds to change in his or her own unique way.

Unfortunately, sometimes church leaders take the attitude, "these resisters are not very spiritual," or they may even think resisters are downright mean or narrow and come to the conclusion that "those people are just in the wrong church." This is normally not the case at all. "Those people" may simply be at a different stage of their reaction to the change than the leaders are. A process of internal transition may have taken the change agent years, yet he or she may be trying to push the church through their transition in a few weeks.

Remember: An effective change agent works through each phase and tries to help other people work through them as well.

➤ Change won't come without trust.

I won't change for you unless I trust you. Church leaders who gather behind closed doors to make decisions, then march out and announce sweeping changes, are asking for trouble. Trust grows out of open, healthy relationships and is nurtured by dialogue.

A seminar on spiritual leadership that I have taught frequently is turning into a book titled *They Smell Like Sheep* (to be released by Howard Publishing Company). The thesis: shepherds smell like sheep because they constantly touch sheep. That's why the sheep will follow them. They trust their shepherd to lead them into green pastures and beside still waters. Good leaders (good change agents) build trust through authentic relationships by serving, loving, listening, laughing, and crying with their flock.

➤ Change won't come without ownership in the change process.

If I announce a change designed to alter your life without first having gotten your input, you are more likely to balk than to buy in. This does not mean, however, that visionaries lead only by group consensus or by a fully democratic process. Usually, the larger a planning task force gets, the more inefficient it becomes. As one man observed, "a camel is a horse put together by a large committee." To paraphrase Peter Drucker: the more participatory your visionary leadership style, the smaller your organization will get. Visionaries must cast vision, and leaders must lead; but not without involving those who will be affected by change. Good ears make good leaders. Leaders may listen through focus groups, questionnaire surveys, and many other means. People are more likely to follow a dream when they feel a sense of owner-ship, and more likely to support what they help create.

➤ Change won't come without disequilibrium.

Webster calls disequilibrium "a state of emotional or intellectual imbalance." Although disequilibrium may be uncomfortable, it is not necessarily bad. Even positive changes create disequilibrium. For example, the fact that some of us want children did not diminish the shock when they actually arrived. Our son and daughter-in-law have a three-year-old daughter and an infant son. Although both children were planned, that second baby shot their dise-quilibrium factor off the charts!

Churches can feel this too. When you change too many things in my church too fast and hold that pace too long, even if I voted enthusiastically for the change, I may eventually dig in my heels.

Somewhere along the way, I cooked up a little antibi-otic for disequilibrium: two facts and two strategies.

Fact one

Change does not come without disequilibrium.

Fact two

People cannot endure *sustained* disequilibrium! Here is where most eye-on-the-goal, can't-wait-for-the-plod-ders style of change agents mess up. They push people into acute disequilibrium and hold them there till an ex-plosion comes. So, what to do?

Strategy one

Weave! Alternate between safety and disequilibrium. Teach new ideas a while, stretching your church out beyond comfort zones and into fresh thinking. At first you may hear, "Wow! I never noticed that in the Bible before!" This is only mild disequilibrium. But when you feel your church approaching the limits of tolerance, back off! Talk about familiar and safe things for a while. Then, move back out to the cutting edge again. Weave out and in—weave out with new ideas, then weave back in with talk of comfortable things. Then weave out again by implementing new practices; then weave back to some old practices that feel safer. Weave! Two steps forward and one step back.

Strategy two

Employ prayerful brinkmanship! Be sensitive and prayerful as you take your church to the brink of change. Watch out! It is immoral to gamble with the solidarity of a church. Don't plunge recklessly toward the brink. *Prayerful* brinkmanship comes back to the key importance of relationship. I dare not lead a church along the brink unless I am very much in touch with the feelings of those people.

During my last few years at the Highland church, I finished my Doctorate of Ministry degree and wrote a book. Overcommitment underdescribes those days. During that time we implemented several major changes at once. People began to murmur. Some locked their brakes. Advisors told us, "Slow down, Lynn. This is too much too fast!"

I defended, "Aw, come on. Don't be nervous. I know these people. I'm listening!" But I really didn't know their feelings. I had gradually withdrawn into my own little world of overcommitment and distraction, oblivious to how far I had drifted out of touch with the church. In addition, by being unavailable for normal daily social interaction, I had made too few deposits in my trust account and was nearly overdrawn.

Trust is crucial in the change process. We are change agents. So was Jesus. But, even Jesus changed people by building trust through relationships. He still does. We are not likely to improve on his approach!

➤ Change won't come unless options are maintained.

I know a number of urban churches that abruptly canceled their Sunday night services—boom—and substituted small groups in homes. It seemed perfectly logical. Sunday night services fit well in the rural, nineteenth-century culture, but their purpose seemed unclear in a late twentieth-century urban setting.

True! But, some people still feel guilty if they don't come to the church building on Sunday nights, and they may view the cancellation as a step away from God. However, some congregations employed a more effective strategy. When they switched to small groups in homes on Sunday evenings, they also maintained a "nongroup" small group at the church building. They maintained options.

Another example: Years back, at the Highland Church of Christ in Abilene, Texas, we began singing occasionally during what had traditionally been a silent communion reflection. Some loved it. Others smelled heresy! So we devised options. One Sunday we would say, "In this church Christians love to help each other worship. Some of us prefer silent reflection during the communion. So today the rest of us are going to love those people and reflect silently with them. But next Sunday, we will sing during communion, and those who prefer silence will love those who like singing." In this case, we alternated between two options.

Unfortunately, sometimes the folks that have been around a congregation the longest have the most control and tend to force their way on what is often the larger group of more recent members. But love does not force one group of people to another group's comfort zones. Maintaining options along with changes diminishes friction.

➤ Change won't come immediately!

Back in the early days of our nineteen years at the Highland church, some of the elders and I prayed and worked towards changes that didn't happen until *fifteen years later!* Be patient.

Besides, pushing for immediate changes can backfire. Suppose that, on a scale of one to ten, I want to change a church from a two to a nine. Being a type-A person, I may consider myself a patient change agent if I only shoot for an eight the first time. However, trying to go that far in one fell swoop may actually drive the congregation backwards to a hardened minus fourteen! A more effective strategy might be to shoot for a five on the first attempt, and then celebrate progress if the group only makes it to a three on that round.

Some of my aged-peers and I have tried to be change agents for over thirty years. Significant progress has been made, but not yet all we'd hope for. Some younger than we are God's change agents too. Still others will come after them. God did not appoint any one generation to single-handedly do the changes for all of history. No rush. Let God choose the timing. Celebrate the progress instead of lamenting the frustration. Besides, if you ever get things the way you want them, some young Turk will come along and change it all anyway. Let us echo the Alcoholics Anonymous' serenity prayer:

> Lord grant me the serenity
> To accept the things I cannot *change,*
> The courage to *change* the things I can
> And the wisdom to know the difference.[4]

➤ Change won't come permanently without maintenance!

People forget. New Year's resolutions seldom make it until March. We must regularly reexplain why changes are made. People need to be re-reminded of the reasons the new way is better. The biblical rationale for change must be repeated at regular intervals because we forget.

Good maintenance clearly spells out the parameters of change and frequently reviews them: "We will do this, but not do that. We will go this far and no farther. We will experiment this long, and then reevaluate." This reduces fear of change.

Maintenance is also needed because of turnover. A few years back, a trio of girls sang a communion reflection on Sunday morning—which we had often done previously, but not for some months. You would have thought the bad place had busted loose! A wave of new members had joined us since we had last used this singing format. They had not heard our rationale. What was old hat to most of us shocked the newcomers. A bit of maintenance might have brought the new folks up to speed and spared us all the trauma.

I am painfully aware of my own personal need for maintenance. You too, right? I clean up my act, then before long, I drift. (Thank God for his patience!) If individuals need maintenance, surely groups do too.

➤ Change will not come completely.

That's human nature. Although I've been a Christian since high school, I am still wondering if I'll ever realize some changes in my life that I have been working on for years. I really do *want* to change, and I am changing, gradually, but never completely. If individuals never change completely, why expect it of groups? The church is, after all, only a collection of blemished individuals.

Most urban churches experience constant turnover. For some months now, new families have joined our congregation nearly every Sunday. People leave as well. Consequently, change will never completely keep pace with turnovers.

Finally, change will not come completely as long as the culture keeps changing. If we stay in touch with the culture, new church formats and approaches will have only a limited shelf life.

➤ Change may not be ethical in some situations.

Some of us may be forced to hard choices. You may be driven by a passion to reach totally unchurched seekers or by a concern to keep from losing the boomer or buster generation from the church. But these people are not likely to be reached through traditional church models. You may have tried your best to get your congregation to retool so that it can connect with the unchurched or with a new generation of Christians. But others in your church, maybe even the founders who have invested their life's blood in your congregation, may be driven by a different vision. In that case, to force your changes may not be ethical.

All churches don't have to be the same. Some churches can change a little, some a lot. I expect to see a lot more changes in the future because we are learning better change skills and strategies. We are also sifting what really needs to change from the merely cosmetic changes. But remember, some churches won't be able to change— not at all! Attempts to force 180 degree changes on such churches simply is not ethical. If you are a member of such a church, but you feel driven by a vision that does not fit your congregation, it may be best for you to say, "Brothers, would you help me plant a new church over yonder? I must do this in order to follow God's calling for me." Whether your home congregation chooses to help you or not, *you* have no God-given choice but to keep on loving and respecting them and to follow your call and your conscience into some other ministry setting.

Enthusiasm for new church plantings is on the rise. For example, each year, larger percentages of students in my graduate courses want to be church planters. However, the central legitimate motivation for planting new churches is a God-given vision that cannot be accomplished "where you are now." A passion and dream to plant a church is no reflection on your home church. It may simply mean that your vision does not fit your church's life cycle. The first generation of a new church is usually highly evangelistic and clearly focused. But, as a church gathers additional "constituencies," it may become less militant and single-minded, but better at nurturing or sending. Rather than being critical of such churches, let's celebrate their strengths.

All this talk of change is not a criticism of our past. Remember: It simply means we feel a passion to (1) connect with unchurched people, (2) worship authentically in the heart language of today's culture, and (3) effectively change lives. Yet, we must move cautiously, lest in our push to connect we surrender something precious. (See the appendixes for readings on change agency.)

Look at the stars. Taurus, Pegasus, Orion, and the others move each hour of the night, rotating around the north star, but *the north star never moves.* For centuries, sailors have steered safely to harbor, guided by that one fixed star. Everything is changing, but Jesus Christ is the same yesterday, today, and forever. As my friend David Lusk says, "Let changes come. They must come. But let the north star remain fixed, and all is well!"

When leaders introduce
one change after another,
without allowing time
for internal *transition,*
resistance usually sets in.

CHAPTER TWELVE

*T*RANSITION OR JUST CHANGE?

Wise change agents do not attempt to force unwanted change, but rather serve as navigational leaders who help and guide and provide understanding. The voyage can be exciting and fulfilling, but not likely without mishap. This chapter lays out more navigational instruments to help guide your journey through change.

Two concepts, featured repeatedly in this discussion—*change* and *transition*—are crucial to understanding.

William Bridges, author of *Managing Transitions* and a change consultant for corporations, churches, and career changes, distinguishes in a helpful way between change and transition: *Change* is what happens "out there." Change is moving into a new house or to a new church building. Change is dropping Sunday night services at the church building in favor of small groups in homes. It is introducing a worship-leading team in place of the traditional single leader or switching from the traditional hymns from a songbook to new songs projected on a screen or dropping a denominational church name and using a local community designation. Change is *external.*

Transition, on the other hand, says Bridges, is the *internal,* personal process triggered by the external change, the psychological reorientation to the new arrangement. Transition requires *time* and is handled by different people in different ways. But the egg hits the fan when change occurs without the necessary personal transition. Most of us have experienced this. Wham! The company moves us. Or the elders change the hour of worship. Or the minister resigns. And we have no time to adjust psychologically to the change. Problems with change in a church and other organizations are not usually over change itself. The problems are usually over *lack of transition.* When leaders continue to introduce one change after another without providing help and allowing time for internal transition, resistance usually sets in.

Bridges also observes that healthy transitions need *endings, neutral zones,* and *new beginnings.*

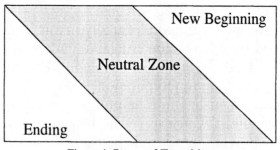

Figure 4. **Stages of Transition**
Adapted from William Bridges[1]

Bridges likens internal transition to the biblical Exodus story. Phase one is "leaving Egypt," *ending* the familiar way of life. He insists that people need endings to "the way it was"—to old routines, roles, relationships, and comfortable traditions.

The second phase of transition is the "wilderness wanderings," or the *neutral zone.* This in-between time is often chaotic, with a potent mixture of possibility and threat. But the wilderness can also be a time of reflection, assessment, and midcourse correction. It is absolutely imperative that the neutral zone be managed well, or people may retreat to the old way. And once people retrench, mounting a second change effort will be infinitely more difficult than launching the first.

Bridges' third phase of transition is the "promised land," or the *new beginning.* It is characterized by new terrain, new identity, and new roles. People in this phase are no longer slaves or wanderers, but landholders. A healthy new beginning can also be an exciting time for fresh commitments. Thus, during new beginnings, a church may experience a burst of energy.

As we continue through this material, remember that change navigation is more an art than a science. Bridges' model is only a way of seeing, a model. It is not intended to be scientifically precise, much less etched in stone. However, as one ponders the parallels between the exodus and organizational change, practical implications keep popping up. Let's look at the stages of transition a little more closely.

ENDING

"Leaving Egypt" is like running the bases: you can't steal second without leaving first base. Or, ending can be seen as a kind of unfreezing period. If you want to change the shape of a lump of ice, say, from a cube to a pyramid shape, you could use the bigger-hammer approach like Tim the Tool-man and crush it to powder, then reassemble it in another shape. Or you could melt the cube, pour the water into a pyramid-shaped mold, and refreeze it.

Some of my change agent attempts have fizzled because we began without *doing an ending*. Bam! Just like that! This abrupt style is all too common in churches. So, how do congregational leaders do an ending? How do you get the people to leave Egypt? There are several things you can do.

➤ Acknowledge their losses.

Make sure people understand that you (the change agents) appreciate the significance of their losses. Ask, "Who is losing what?" And genuinely hear the answer!

➤ Compensate for the losses.

What kind of trade-off can be offered. For example, Carey Garrett's company recently promoted her from leading a change management team into a new job that requires a lot of travel. To compensate for Carey's lack of enthusiasm for the travel, they allow her to work out of her home when she is in town.

In our church when the nursery preempted the space of Adults #2, Adults #2 got a classroom which, while less convenient, is much larger—a nice trade-off.

➤ Communicate a vision of what is ahead.

Answer their questions as thoroughly as possible. "What might the promised land look like?" "What are the benefits of getting there?" This helps give people the confidence to make the leap.

➤ Get people involved in the change.

Good change navigators help people to "own" part of the development of the vision, so they can see what it will be like on the other side of the river. It also diminishes their fears since they retain some feeling of control over their destiny.

➤ Give people lots of information.

Overkill is almost impossible. People need to know specifically what will and will not change. Some change agents simply get frustrated with X and want change *now,* any change, to escape X. So they recklessly push ahead rather than patiently transitioning the system. They change things they *don't* like before they know exactly what they *do* like, with no compelling rationale for the change and no clear picture of where the change will take them. After all, being forced to leave home without a clear destination feels a lot like being kidnapped! People want to know the parameters and benefits. Change must be driven by a compelling, carefully planned, strategic rationale, not merely blind frustration. Again, information is crucial. Think of the most information you could ever communicate and then triple that. Information helps diminish the shock of endings.

➤ **Show how precious values will be preserved in spite of the change.**

Even secular organizations try to carry values through transitions. How much more important that Christian people feel confident that their core values are not only being preserved through the changes, but that proposed change in their church will more effectively perpetuate, communicate, and apply the core values of the faith. When it comes down to it, the only valid reason to change things in a church is precisely to better preserve and perpetuate core values. That is, to keep "the faith once for all delivered to the saints" (Jude 3).

When Israel was poised to cross the Jordan into the promised land, Joshua calmed their fears of the unknown by reminding them that the most important thing of all would not change.

> *When you see the ark of the covenant of the Lord your God, and the priests who are the Levites, carrying it, you are to move out from your positions and follow it. Then you will know which way to go, since you have never been this way before.* (Josh. 3:3)

In other words, "Get ready! Everything is going to change—except God. He is still our God, and we are still his people."

➤ **Provide closure to what is ending.**

You can do this through celebrations and ceremonies— even with symbolic gestures. For example, the new president of one corporation was making his company less hierarchical and more empowering. So, he called a news conference and personally painted out the president's "reserved" parking spot. He circulated a video tape of the ceremony through all departments. This sent a strong "closure" signal.

Some kinds of closing ceremonies are old hat in churches: funerals, graduation ceremonies, going-away parties, bond burnings, even weddings.

In one church where I served, the elders relieved from her duties a Sunday school supervisor with twenty years of tenure. However, they designed a Sunday evening service in her honor, highlighting reminiscences from former coteachers and students, and presented her with a plaque. This ending ceremony sweetened the bitter pill for her, and at the same time, sent a clear closure message to the congregation.

NEUTRAL ZONE

The next phase is the wilderness wanderings (or neutral zone). *Beginnings* got the people out of Egypt. The *neutral zone* gets the Egypt out of the people.

Of course, that in-between, neutral-zone time is usually a bit dangerous, but several strategies can help you navigate the neutral zones.

➤ Provide opportunities for personal communication.

During this time of instability and fear, there will be more need than ever for ample communication. But neutral-zone communication must be more personal than was ending communication. People will want to bend the ears of their leaders, so leaders will need to be out and about, available to people. William Bridges slightly modifies the Tom Peters' concept of MBWA ("management by walking around") for the neutral zone to "Moses been wandering around." In the neutral zone, people want their

"Moses" to be available, and to feel that he is with them in the uncertainty of wandering.

Thus, the neutral zone is *not* the time for leaders to hide from the nay-sayers. Rather, it is a time to sit down around the coffee cup in Bible classes, backyards, and living rooms, involving all constituencies in the reflective and creative process of listening, dialoging, clarifying— and yes, sometimes even modifying.

➤ Put temporary structures in place.

You are no longer doing things like you did them in Egypt, and you're not yet sure how you will do them in the promised land, so temporary structures help stabilize things.

For example, a couple of years ago our congregation totally revamped its way of appointing elders. Historically, at Preston Road, the elders themselves had selected whomever they felt qualified, whenever they chose to do so, by announcing their appointments to the congregation. But the congregation changed. Approximately 80 percent had become members within the previous four years. So the elders, feeling they no longer represented the new church, handed the selection process to the entire congregation.

The temporary structures for this neutral zone were two ad hoc committees of men and women from a cross section of the congregation. The first committee *designed* a plan for congregational participation in elder selection. The second committee *implemented* the plan. But once the new elders were in place, the temporary committees disbanded.

➤ **Tap the creativity within the group.**

People are breaking out of old ways of doing and seeing things. New insights may flourish. Creativity often soars. This is all the more reason for leaders to ask, listen, and empower during this phase of transition.

Warning: Attempts to move too quickly through the neutral zone may create a trust and credibility deficit for leaders, and you may run the risk of frightening people back into an even more resistant old way—just as the children of Israel murmured when Moses moved too fast for them and begged to return to the security of slavery in Egypt. Leaders must keep constantly in touch with where people are on the transition continuum in order to choose appropriate timing.

NEW BEGINNING

The last phase is the *new beginning,* as we enter the Promised Land. You are now making the external change—moving into the new building, or beginning the Sunday-evening small groups, or trading your song leader for a worship-leading team with contemporary music and without hymnals. Or you are shifting the Bible school from Sunday morning to Sunday night or ordaining a new minister next Sunday. Life in the promised land!

What strategies are helpful now?

➤ **Ample communication is needed.**

Communication is necessary every step of the way. People are now looking for information on what the future will look like: "Give me a detailed plan." "What are the milestones?" "Exactly what is my new role?"

➤ Build in small wins.

Stop and celebrate any bit of concrete progress. This reassures supporters and helps bring along the skeptics. When our congregation underwent some classroom, nursery, and office changes, we made the changes gradually, giving people time to adjust, and celebrated each addition or move with a grand opening and special tour.

➤ Build in time-outs.

People can endure only so much change at one time. Some leaders ignore this, to their regret. For example, one congregation launched into a laundry list of "eleven initiatives," all equally important, all to be implemented at once. To avert disaster, wiser heads persuaded the change task force to back off and prioritize. Then after the implementation of each new "initiative," the church took a breather, celebrated the gains, and allowed people's internal transitions to catch up.

Endings, neutral zones, new beginnings—each is a necessary step.

PORTRAIT OF A TRANSITION

An excellent example of healthy transition through these phases is the Highland Church of Christ in Abilene, Texas, when, in 1990–91 they changed ministers. I had stood in the Highland pulpit for nineteen very happy years; and after resigning from the pulpit, I remained on staff for another year, writing and doing church consulting. It was not a dismissal nor a forced resignation nor an angry departure. It simply seemed to Carolyn and me that God was bringing that chapter of our ministry to a healthy conclusion. Still, the transition was very painful for me,

Carolyn, and the congregation. However, the church moved through an unusually healthy yearlong transition process.

The ending was formalized by three "ceremonies." The first ending ceremony came the day I announced my resignation. Even now, after more than three years, as I write these words, my eyes mist over, and separation pain stabs my heart. I feel the shocked expressions, tears, hugs, and, of course, some denial—even some resistance. The second ceremony was a going-away party the church threw for us. After the morning service, we adjourned to the Family Life Center for a receiving line of well-wishing, accompanied by punch, cake, and festivities. By this time, people were feeling less hurt and rejected. They were beginning to understand how this change could be positive.

The third ceremony occurred the Sunday morning I preached my last sermon at Highland. By this time most of us were adjusting to the reality of the ending. The day was still painful, but the ending had been formalized, and we had all been allowed time to grieve our losses.

Then came the neutral zone. The church chose not to secure a new minister for a year. Several of the elders and some deacons did the preaching. Randy Becton, Glen Owen, Paul Faulkner, Charles Siburt, Jimmy Mankin, Tom Milholland, John Willis, Bruce Davis, Carroll Osburn, and others led throughout the "wilderness" year.

During that year, the Highland Church also did a thorough self-study, asking: Who is the Highland church? Where are we going next? What kind of person do we want in our pulpit? Focus groups abounded. Rivers of communication flowed between the congregation and her leaders.

Then, a year later, when Mike Cope became their minister, the Highland church ceremonialized their new beginning. John Allen Chalk, who had served that church for four years prior to my twenty-year tenure, and I were invited back home for a special "Mike Cope Ordination Sunday." John Allen and I spoke brief messages and then "handed the gavel" on to Mike. The elders gave Mike a charge, laid hands on him, and ordained him as their new minister; and Mike painted his dream for the future.

With fervent prayer, tears of nostalgia, and tears of joyful anticipation, the Highland church launched into its new beginning, and the assembly was dismissed to a banquet in Cope's honor. Here, John Allen and I reminisced over some humorous and touching pivotal moments from the past, as did several of the elders. Externally, Highland *changed* ministers, but much more importantly, they managed an internal *transition* in a very healthy and positive way.

STRATEGIES THAT APPLY THROUGHOUT ALL STAGES

In additions to strategies peculiar to each of the three phases, some principles apply all across the entire process.

➤ Pray.

Both change agents and the congregation must bathe their deliberations in constant prayer. Prayer sensitizes us to our own motives and makes us sensitive to the perceptions of others and, of course, more alert to the leading of God. Besides, God has promised that if we ask for wisdom he will not withhold it (James 1:5).

➢ Change only those things critical to the objectives of the church.

Needless changes deplete your trust account and burn credibility needed for critical issues. Prioritize changes, so that you can implement them one at a time, in order of their importance. Remember, people only have a certain capacity for change. So we must be economical with changes, not overdrawing the tolerance accounts of our members.

Carey Garrett says, "If you change too many things too fast, people get the 'kidney stone' mentality, which is 'If only I hold on long enough, this too shall pass.'"

➢ Provide ample theological rationale for changes all through the process.

In healthy evangelical churches, the Bible gets people's attention. A compelling biblical rationale for each proposed change will shift perceptions more effectively than any other strategy. We have no business making any change in a church for which we have no biblical rationale! The word is "a lamp to my feet and a light for my path" (Ps. 119:105). This should precede and then undergird the change process. We must not pull verses from Scripture to sloganize the change, but rather we must teach major theological themes and their implications for change.

➢ Constantly communicate the strategic benefits of proposed change.

Again, it is scarcely imaginable that there could be any such thing as overcommunication during transitions. However, the communication media and strategy will need to gradually, but steadily, shift through the stages of transition. In the early stages, communication can be less personal in the form of one-way public announcements such as, "Some general thought is being given to . . ."

In the neutral zone and on into the new beginning, communication should become increasingly personal and two-way. The general idea is mapped in the following graphic:

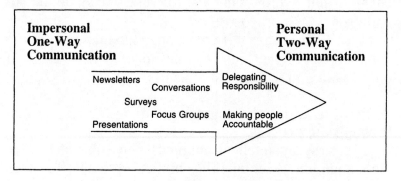

Figure 5. **Communication Continuum**

➤ **Continually assess.**

Be sure at each step that the church has the capability to make the proposed change.

➤ **Constantly nourish and model an environment of trust, collaboration, cooperation, openness, and learning.**

➤ **Consistently model the changes.**

By modeling the changes, leaders will reenforce the new way. Here is a clear example of how *not* to model change: Some weeks back we changed the time and format of our office staff meetings. As with most changes, the new system began raggedly, with people tardy because they "forgot the new time." I climbed all over our staff about coming late to meetings. Well, guess who was the next guy to come late? Not a good way to model change!

➤ Respect people's need to move through each stage at their own pace.

Don't forget that you, the change agent, may have progressed to the neutral zone or the new beginnings phase, while others may still be way back in Egypt. Peter Maris, author of *Loss and Change,* underscores this in the following quote. Read it over carefully two or three times:

> No one can resolve the crisis of reintegration on behalf of another. When those who have power to manipulate changes act as if they have only to explain, and when their explanations are not at once accepted, shrug off opposition as ignorance or prejudice, they express a profound contempt for the meaning of lives other than their own. For the reformers have already assimilated these changes to their purposes, and worked out a reformulation which makes sense to them, perhaps through months or years of analysis and debate. If they deny others the chance to do the same, they treat them as puppets dangling by the threads of their own conceptions.[2]

Reread that second sentence! If those in power "shrug off opposition as ignorance," they show a "profound contempt for the meaning of lives other than their own." Somehow the words, "Do unto others as you would have them do unto you" come to mind here!

Effective church leadership will lovingly, patiently help congregations progress through these stages. No stage can be skipped or ignored. Each person's internal transitioning is unique. Every one of us has our own perceptions of a given change that affects our ability to end what we are now, get through the neutral zone, and move on to a new beginning.

If we operate from a warped mental map, we will surely lose our way.

CHANGING PERCEPTIONS

Flag this chapter. It brings us to what Carey Garret and I see as the single most important ingredient in successful change navigation: *understanding perceptions.* A dear friend and colleague, Dr. Bob Scott, frequently reminds me that perceptions are reality. For no one is this axiom more crucial than for change navigators. A change navigator who ignores the power of perceptions is likely to run his ship aground.

DEFINING PERCEPTIONS

And, what do we mean by *perception?* Perception is the way we see things. It is our interpretation of reality. Several things influence this interpretation: Our collective *cultural* (this can be a religious culture) values, experiences, assumptions, and beliefs, and our own *personal* values, experiences, assumptions, and beliefs. Perceptions (interpreted reality) are like mental maps or models. And charting our course by the wrong map—a distorted perception—will lead us in the wrong direction. Imagine trying to lead a parade through New York City by following a map of Denver. Trying harder won't get you where you want to go; good efforts will still produce wrong results because your map doesn't fit reality.

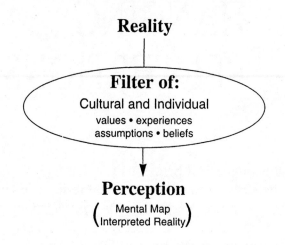

Figure 6. **Perception Equals Filtered Reality**

This figure shows how our filter of cultural and individual experiences, assumptions, and beliefs influences our perception. If we operate from a warped mental map, we will surely lose our way!

When strategies for congregational change are built on mental maps, models, or perceptions that are not *tested* for accuracy, we will not reach our destination. We test our perceptions by (1) reexamining our original data, and (2) by "comparing notes" with a number of respected people. For example, your mental map may say: "Reaching unchurched people is job one!" (your perception of the congregation's values), and "Contemporary music and dramatic skits in assemblies will connect with unchurched people" (your perception of what works). While the congregation may verbalize evangelism as first priority, you may learn while testing your perceptions that the internalized priority for the church may be security, held in place by tradition. Besides, in your setting, contemporary music may not be the best way to connect with unchurched people. Thus, even though you may understand systems and transitions, your strategy is built on major misperceptions and will produce ineffective outcomes. What you thought would please the church and connect with the unchurched may actually offend the churched and repel the unchurched. Outcome: Your church would likely double-shrink!

Thus, at its most crucial point, *change is about perceptions.* Change management is perception management.

OLD AND NEW PERCEPTIONS

Note the contrast, in our rapidly changing times, between old perceptions and new perceptions. Some old perceptions of reality that dominated either the distant or more recent past might be the following:

- The earth is flat. This perception controlled global exploration until Columbus drew a new mental map.
- Women have no right to vote.

- An employment career is lifelong, with a company that will take care of you. (Few baby boomers assume this nowadays.)

Some old perceptions about churches might be these:
- No people know the Bible like our people!
- Public schools help parents reinforce moral values.
- The Bible commands that we must only sing congregationally in worship assemblies.
- Revivals and door knocking and hand-out tracts are the most effective evangelistic methods.
- Take a moment and jot in the margin some additional old perceptions that come to your mind.

Some new perceptions, on the other hand, include the following:
- Capitalism is possible in communistic countries—new in the last five years!
- Nelson Mandella and F. W. deKlerk could share the Nobel Peace Prize.
- Responsibility for employment lies with the individual. Just this year, business-oriented magazines including *Business Week* and *Fortune* play a common theme: "You are responsible for your career. You can't expect big companies to take care of you. These days businesses often have shorter life cycles than do careers." Conversely, in today's climate, companies cannot expect to keep employees merely by promising security.

Some new religious perceptions:

- "Ah! I see our people are not the only ones who read the Scriptures."
- Discipleship is more important than membership.
- Spiritual growth is nurtured more effectively in small group relationships than under powerful preaching.
- Evangelism is relational more than confrontational.
- God cares more about substance than he does about form.
- Leaders should liberate and empower the people in the pews rather than make decisions and withhold or grant permissions.
- Loyalty no longer holds people to a particular church. Since baby boomers shop for convenience, price, and quality—rather than familiar brand names at favorite stores—churches can no longer build their future on "brand name" or congregational loyalty. People will not keep attending a Church of Christ or a Baptist church or a Presbyterian church simply because their parents did, for the name brand, or for its "doctrinal correctness." They don't think about lifetime loyalty to a church. They go to a church only as long as it connects and serves their spiritual purposes. When it doesn't, "I'm down the road to one that does." Today's baby boomers expect to make their own choices regarding spiritual and moral development; they do not delegate that to their denomination!

- Interrupt your reading briefly now, and jot down a few personal examples in the margin.

HOW PERCEPTIONS FORM

Another way of looking at the developmental pattern of a perception comes from Chris Argyris. Argyris charts this development on a ladder.

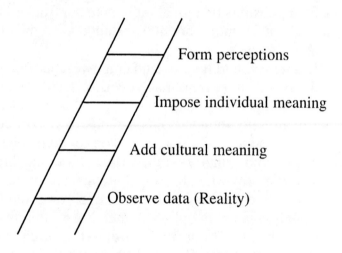

Form perceptions

Impose individual meaning

Add cultural meaning

Observe data (Reality)

Figure 7. **Perception Formation**
Adapted from Chris Argyris[1]

First, we *observe actual data.* Data is picked up through channels such as what is actually said in a conversation or communicated through body language that you observe—for example, you may observe that a man's face turned red. Data can also take the form of widely agreed upon history, statistics, or trends—for example, statistics tell us that church growth has declined X percent in the last X years. We usually have fairly objective data when most people, regardless of their culture or personal background, agree on the data. The Bible is the core source of sound spiritual data and a common ground for developing shared perceptions.

Second, we *add cultural meaning*, which is colored by a number of elements, such as our church roots or the country we're from. For example, our cultural interpretation of a red face is that it indicates anger.

Third, we *impose individual meanings* based on our own personal life experiences and upbringing. For example, I may believe that anger is unhealthy and unprofitable.

Fourth, we *form perceptions* or theories. These perceptions or mental maps are generated from our understanding of reality. Of course, these perceptions, in turn, determine our actions. For example, I may perceive that withdrawing from or avoiding this angry person is the most appropriate response.

Here's a riddle that's another example of the power of perceptions. John leaves home and makes three stops, but he doesn't get back home because of the man with the mask. Question: where did John go?

Did the man with the mask have a gun? Did John drop by the grocery, the pharmacy, and the laundry? Was John waylaid by a car-jacker in the parking lot? These mental models usually come first to mind.

But watch the mental-model instantly shift when we think "baseball diamond." John hits a triple, but the "masked man" tagged him out at home plate. (If we had said it was Jill that left home, our perceptions would have misled us even further.)

Note that we first heard basic data: the man left home. Then we added cultural meanings congruent with our sensitivity to street crime. Then we imposed our individual meaning—and abracadabra—we pulled a perception out of the hat. The original data (reality) was then filtered through our influences so that we perceived a baseball game to be a mugging.

Let us revisit an earlier illustration of the way perceptions affect worship forms and evangelistic strategies.

1. *We observed data:* Our religious fathers deemed it appropriate to hold Sunday night services at the church building. Many of us are unaware that an early minister began holding Sunday night services to capitalize on the crowds of country folks who gathered to see the new gas lights in his town. It worked! Other ministers saw that Sunday evenings "worked," so the practice spread, gathering perceptions as time went on.

2. *We added cultural meaning to the data:* "Sunday night church services are an effective evangelistic outreach." Therefore, churches across the country adopted this strategy.

3.*We imposed individual meaning:* Going to church on Sunday nights reflects on my commitment to the Lord.

4. *We formed the perception* that Sunday night services held at the church building are essential. This perception now persists as an old mental map by which we determine our course of action in today's world. After we slid Bible verses under our perception, it escalated from *the* way to do things to the way *God* wants it done, so that now in some churches, Sunday evening services are mandatory. Consequently, when an urban church today wants to change its church calendar and replace traditional Sunday

night services with some alternative like Sunday-night house churches, that church's soundness comes under question.

But the culture keeps changing, so that our old perceptions (formed from old data and passed through an old filter) distort new contextual reality even more! Strategies built on these old perceptions are understandably ineffective. This has happened with whole constellations of church strategies, programs, events, vocabularies, and even beliefs.

The larger and older a church, the more likely it will resist change, because older institutions are composed of intertwined layers of long-standing collective perceptions and mental maps drawn using old and filtered data. However, like the proverbial frog in the kettle, the church is often unaware that the surrounding culture is changing slowly, gradually—but drastically—so that the church smoothly and predictably drifts into irrelevance and out of meaningful connections with the culture. Without some intervention, many churches are moving comfortably on precisely this course—toward eventual oblivion!

Yes, as my friend Dr. Scott says, perceptions are reality. They are not abstract ideas inside our heads; but they affect what we say and what we do. They determine strategies and outcomes.

HOW PERCEPTIONS AFFECT STRATEGIES

Carey Garrett illustrates it this way, "My perception that my husband won't help prepare meals affects my strategies with him. I do all the preparation and get upset because he hasn't helped. That, of course, affects the outcome. He is less likely to help and more likely to become upset himself when I am angry because he 'won't' help. Then his reaction only reinforces my mental model, or perception, that he won't help.

"But the root problem may be in my mental model, the perceptions I hold of my husband, *not* primarily in the strategies I use. If I changed my perception to be, 'He really does want to help, but needs directions on how to help,' then instead of doing it all myself, I would probably approach him nondefensively, specifically asking him if he would like to make a salad or grill the steak. If this resulted in his cheerful and willing partnership in the kitchen work, the outcome would confirm my altered perception, so I would likely continue holding it."

A common assumption or perception in the western management world—and thus in the church—is that leaders know the right things to do. Therefore, leaders decide what is going to happen. Then leaders employ persuasive strategies to help people see the benefits of what the leaders want to do. The inevitable concerns and natural demonstrations of resistance are considered invalid by the leaders. So the leaders' strategy is to build a persuasive case and sell the change.

But when people feel they are being pressed to "buy in" without being asked their input, at best they comply; but they do not feel true commitment or ownership. More often they resist srongly. The resulting resistance matches the "manager's" original misperception and reenforces his mental model that the people just don't know what is good for them. This point was graphically stated in an Associated Press cartoon during the height of the Vietnam War. President Lyndon Johnson was on the phone complaining to his aide, "What's wrong with them

Vietnamese? Don't they realize I'm killin' 'em for their own good?" This kind of mindset steps up intensity and sells harder. Consequently, the change agent learns little from this exchange, nor does the church. Both only become further entrenched in their perceptions. Remember that effective leaders do not "manipulate" or "manage" people or change, they serve merely as loving navigational guides.

As navigational guides, leaders would do well to reexamine their own original perceptions rather than intensifying the persuasion campaign to overpower the resistance and "manage a change." A healthier perception might be, "We don't hold a corner on understanding. Let's get the people involved in the change process. Their thoughts and ideas will enhance our mental maps and may produce very different strategies." The outcomes then may be both emotional and intellectual ownership by the church and full cooperation in implementing or navigating change.

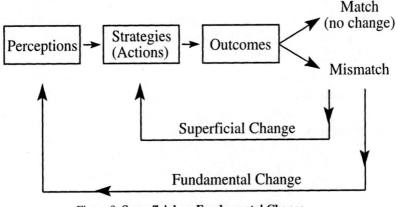

Figure 8. **Superficial vs. Fundamental Change**
Adapted from Chris Argyris[2]

In his book, *Overcoming Organizational Defenses,* Chris Argyris spells out in depth how perceptions affect the strategies and actions we use and how these, in turn, affect the resulting outcomes we get.

If the outcome matches our original perception that resistance simply confirms that people don't know what's good for them, we will likely keep believing and doing the same things (strategies or actions), and the outcome is that no change occurs.

However, when there is a mismatch between our perceptions and our outcomes, our first reaction is usually to try a new strategy or approach, rather than to reexamine our perceptions. "Hmm! Looks like I'll have to change my approach with this person to get my point across" (or with this church to get my change adopted). This leads to *superficial change,* and we keep recycling our old perceptions. Sometimes a light goes off in our head and our new actions eventually lead us to a new perception. But often, after we see that our new reactions aren't working, we eventually revert back to our old actions. Unless we revisit and revise our perceptions, we won't genuinely learn how to change. To get at the root of things, we must go back and reexamine our perceptions, the mental maps that steer the strategies. When we actually start from the beginning and change our perceptions, we will be on our way to *fundamental change* and may learn to move from manipulator to navigator.

With Chris Argyris's perception–strategies–outcomes graphic in our minds, let's suppose that I hold the following three perceptions:

    1. Everybody in our church holds evangelizing the unchurched as the top priority of this church.

    2. Contemporary music in our assemblies is the most
effective way to connect with the unchurched.

    3. It is my responsibility to get things changed.

Based on these perceptions, my strategy may be, "Tell
'em my reasons this week and start the contemporary
music next week."

But when the inevitable uproar ensues, I wonder what
went wrong. *First,* I may have wrongly perceived the
church's perceptions and therefore used the wrong strategies. I didn't look deeply enough to see that their verbalized values were not their real values. They may not agree
that evangelizing the unchurched is a higher priority than
worship and nurture. What they may really value is the
status quo for themselves and their grandchildren. They
may not believe that worship assemblies are for evangelism. And they may think their unchurched friends would
be offended by "this new stuff." *Second,* they may not
perceive me as an "authorized change agent" for their
church nor trust my ability to "manage" change.

Third, I may be out of touch with my own perceptions.
I may have misperceived my own motives for wanting the
change. Deep down, maybe I want contemporary music
because of my own musical taste, or because I want to be
considered "in" by certain of my colleagues, or because I
want to win a power struggle with the old guard. And perhaps some of us old preachers simply feel younger when
we sing youthful music!

Finally, I may have perceived myself as a *change
agent* rather than a *change navigator.*

If I do not reflect on my own perceptions and dialogue
my way into the perceptions of others, redoubling my efforts will only generate more resistance/compliance and

little or no ownership/commitment. In fact, I may only further convince the flock that I am a misguided and impetuous shepherd. And I will have learned nothing. I will have only caused many heartaches! My best solution to this dilemma will not be to devise another strategy, but to begin authentic conversation! (This will be explored in chapter fourteen.)

How perceptions affect structures

In our efforts to understand all the variables that play into our church system, let us move on to another concept. Two closely connected and very important aspects of a congregational system are *perceptions* and *structures*. Structure is the easier to understand because structures are the visible and concrete manifestation of invisible and abstract perceptions. The following graphic illustrates the relationship between the two.

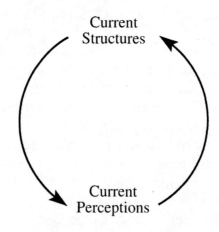

Figure 9. **Perceptions/Structures**

Visible structures are only the tip of the iceberg of a congregational system. The bulk of the system is hidden below the water line. When we walk in the door and look at a congregation, we can see the structures: the way things are done, the physical building, the socio-economic demographic, the style of worship, the symbols and signs, the mood of the color and furnishings, the demeanor of the people, the verbalized values, and other externals. These are the tip of the iceberg. Below the waterline lie the reasons those structures exist: the *perceptions;* and whether the perceptions accurately or inaccurately reflect reality, they are what drives that church. The invisible *why* undergirds the visible *what.*

Notice that Figure 9 maps perceptions and structures in reenforcing circles, showing that perceptions drive structures and that the structures, in turn, reenforce perceptions. These generate a mutually reenforcing or self-perpetuating loop. Some might call it a vicious cycle.

➤ Outdated Perceptions

Think back again to the story about the source of Sunday evening services in small-town nineteenth century America. People flocked from the country to see the gas lights. Preachers seized this evangelistic opportunity. Result: Sunday evening evangelistic preaching. For decades this proved an effective strategy, eventually becoming authentic orthodox structure. So, when rural Christians moved to the cities and planted urban churches, they took the old Sunday night services with them. Today, crowds no longer gather around gas lights, yet we still continue Sunday evening services! The structure still reenforces the old perception that it is important to have Sunday evening meetings at the church house. Thus a perception created a structure which perpetuates a perception, which maintains a structure, which . . . Such loops often keep running long after neither perception nor structure have much to do with current realities.

Understanding how such perceptions come into being might help us break the vicious cycle. Consider the following process:

1950 Reality

Week-long revival
meetings are effective

1950 Filter

Experience:	I saw people brought to Christ during revival meetings.
Values:	I value a method that brings people to Christ.
Belief:	I believe committed people will support revival meetings.
Assumption:	What worked then, will always work.

1990 Outdated Perception

Our church should have
week-long revival meetings.

1990 Reality

People do not attend week-long
revival meetings. Thus they are
no longer effective.

Figure 10. **Outdated Perceptions vs. Current Reality**

➤ Building New Structures

Thus, to initiate transitions that can break a church out of this loop, change agents must clearly envision what they want things to look like in the future and must define new structures that are true to the foundational truths, values, and noble intentions that initiated the obsolete structures before they became obsolete. If we can assure conscientious Christians that our desire for change is not a threat to the fundamental truths of Scripture, we may more readily gain their cooperation and support. What we want to communicate is that while we may be dismantling the old structure and building a new one, the foundational truths and values remain solidly in place. In fact, by evolving the structure, we will probably learn more about the essence of our foundational truths and values.

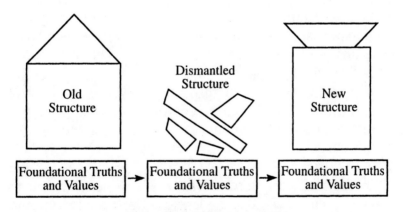

Figure 11. **Dismantling Old Structures**

Assuring our closed-to-change fellow Christians that we revere the same biblical truths they do may modify their perspective of our proposed changes.

➤ Closing the Gap

Effective change agents cannot afford to ignore the gaps between outdated perceptions, current realities, and future vision. The gaps must be recognized, respected, and dealt with.

The formation of dialogue groups can be one step in the gap-closing process. Getting together and talking about what *is*—and why—and about what *could be*—and why—helps each of us discover our own perceptions.

Cautiously modifying structures can also help alter perceptions and close the gaps. In fact, leaders can close the gaps between what is and what ought to be from both sides. For example: Suppose a congregation changes from Sunday night congregational assemblies to meeting in house-church groups. The change agent may attempt to alter perceptions by talking about the value of small groups—defining them, describing parameters, targeting leadership development, listening to testimonies from veterans of effective groups, etc. Then, when at least one effective small group actually begins meeting, the structure itself leads to even further positive perceptions of small groups. So, altered perceptions and new structures facilitate one another. In this case, we have created a "virtuous cycle" rather than the "vicious cycle" we talked about before.

While changing perceptions—ours or someone else's —is not an easy task, understanding how perceptions form and how they affect our strategies and our structures will provide us with helpful tools as we navigate the inevitable winds of change.

The pathway to truth and reality sometimes leads through conflict.

CONVERSATION: WINDOWS INTO PERCEPTIONS

In the previous chapter we observed through the wide-angle lens how our perceptions of reality affect our *strategies* for change. In this chapter we will zoom in and focus on one dimension: how our perceptions of change affect our *conversational* strategies.

As Peter Senge words it: "conversation is an excellent window into our perception of change." My conversational strategies can reveal whether I perceive change to be good or bad, and my *perception* of change will in turn determine whether I am open or closed to change.

What conversational clues do we listen for? Peter Senge cites the subtle but powerful difference between two types of conversation, using the words *discussion* and *dialogue. Discussion* is a grandchild of the word percussion—banging against each other, noisy collision; whereas *dialogue* originates from the idea of *coming through* the conversation to a higher meaning than any one individual could come to alone.

People who perceive change negatively will more likely *discuss* than *dialogue.* They bring to the conversation a resolve not to change their thinking—since the assumption is that "change is bad." Discussion requires only that they communicate *their* ideas, not that they be influenced or changed by the ideas of others. In *discussion,* a person speaks, advocates, influences, persuades, and argues. On the other hand, people who are open to change are bent more toward cooperational dialogue because they enter the conversation open to changing their thinking. Dialogue assumes two-way communication, so it involves listening, as well as speaking, and building on the ideas of others. In dialogue, a person speaks and listens, advocates and inquires, creates trust and openness, and cooperates.

CONVERSATIONAL STRATEGIES

➣ Perceptions Determine Conversational Strategies

Let's revisit Chris Argyris' chart from chapter thirteen (Figure 7), expand on its basic principles, and apply them specifically to conversational strategies.

Underlying Perceptions	
Closed (negative perception of change)	**Open** (positive perception of change)

I am rational
Others are irrational
I must avoid negative feelings
I must "save face"
	I and others can change
	My goals include:
	  Understanding reality
	  Producing valid information
	  Learning foundational
	    truths and values

Conversational Strategies	
Closed (Discussion)	**Open** (Dialogue)
Speaking Advocating Influencing Persuading Selling Arguing	Speaking and listening Advocating and Inquiring Cooperating Creating Willing to have ideas challenged

Outcome	
Closed	**Open**
Defensiveness Manipulation Lack of trust Political game playing Low commitment Miscommunication Inflexibility Ineffectiveness	Open communication Honest communication Flexibility Trust Commitment Effectiveness Collaboration Learning

Figure 12. **Conversational Clues to Perception**

The preceding diagram is not meant to classify people into fixed roles, but to alert us to conversational clues that help us better understand our own perceptions of change. In our discussion, the terms *open to change* and *closed to change* describe general tendencies, not fixed personalities. Of course, all of us balk at change in certain areas of our life, but our underlying perceptions of change significantly affect our overall openness, or lack of openness, to change; and our conversational strategies provide clues to the perceptions of both ourselves and others. Being alert to these clues can help us as we navigate the winds of change.

Underlying Perceptions

We all approach conversation with our own set of underlying perceptions. Those closed to change assume, "I am rational and others are irrational." Our old-time religious debaters often nailed down a point with something like, "Intelligent people will understand that." Or, "That's not *about* it. That's *it!* If not, why not?" The underlying perception was "I am (we are) rational, and anyone who disagrees with me (us) is irrational!"

A current equivalent among would-be change agents would run something like this: "I've studied church growth. I've studied worship and I know what makes a church go. 'They' don't seem to understand. But I do! I am rational and they are not. So I can ignore their input and bulldoze over their resistance."

Another basic perception of closed-to-change people is that negative feelings must be avoided. These people assume that they must keep others feeling good and themselves looking good. Church folk tend to define peace and health in terms of tranquillity, in which no one experiences disturbed feelings and everybody's "face" is saved, no matter how obstructive his or her ideas and behavior might be. This, too, produces congregational family secrets and all the attending systemic dysfunction. (Yes, churches, like families, can be dysfunctional.)

In contrast, the open mindset expects that others can change. The person who perceives change as positive assumes that the most important thing is reality, objectivity, and truth, rather than getting my way or being comfortable. The open person assumes that others too are rational, that they too are interested in truth.

The open-to-change person believes in the value of producing valid information so that people can make informed choices and take personal responsibility for their choices. The bottom line is that this open mindset is interested in discovering reality. It seeks to allow all players to participate in seeking what is true, what is best for all. However, open-to-change people know that sometimes the pathway to truth and reality leads through disagreements; sometimes, even through mild conflict.

Healthy churches are not necessarily those that never experience conflict. Years ago in a seminar on marriage and family, I made the statement that a married couple who says they never fight are either not living together or they are lying! I was confronted in the lobby by an upbeat couple who said they were mildly offended at my remarks. They said they had been married over a decade, were even in business together, but they had *never* had a fight! I suspected that they were either in denial or defined fighting as shouting or getting violent. Unfortunately, both of my suspicions proved to be accurate years later. Acute family dysfunction began to show up. Their bright and gifted son became substance addicted. The daughter became lesbian. Misdirected anger, mistrust, and family secrets flourished.

Some churches, too, that "never fight" meet with deep dysfunction and produce spiritually troubled people. They also tend to lose momentum and slip toward decline because needed corrective changes would require painfully honest dialogue and even conflict.

Conversational Strategies

Since those who are closed to change are not open to changing their own ideas or perceptions, they may assume that others are the ones who need to do all the changing. They believe they are right and have the true answer and must therefore impose it upon other people. The conversational strategy is something like, "If I can't sell 'em, I'll finesse 'em. And if that won't work, I'll just have to roll right over them. But somehow I've got to change them, because they'll never change themselves!" This has been the prevailing mindset of past management in the Western world that most of us have learned by osmosis. "Be in control, especially when you are in a leadership position."

The closed style tends to squelch empowerment of others, while the open style promotes personal discovery and learning, which bestows empowerment. The open person adds essential strategies to those listed on the left side of the chart. The open person speaks *and* listens, he advocates *and* inquires. Open dialogue is cooperational and seeks to create correct information.

I have lost count of the phone calls and letters from frustrated ministers, elders, and others over the last couple of years. One theme keeps coming through: "the rest of the brethren" are not open to change. "They" are closed minded. "There is no use!"

Yes, I think I know our fellowship. And I am not blind to its faults. And I have been on the receiving end of some of its dysfunction. In fact, I have probably produced some dysfunction myself. But in my experience, our fellowship is generally quite open to change. As mentioned earlier, many church leaders who, fifteen to twenty years ago, wrote me up as a heretic, now invite me to speak on their platforms. I haven't changed much; I probably should have changed more than I have. But the church *has* changed—enormously. Frankly, I am weary of hearing the refrain that churches *can't* change, and people *won't* change. I perceive that assumption to be coming from the closed-to-change side of the chart!

This mindset treats others as obstacles to get around or insists that there is something wrong with their spirituality. Whoa!! Brothers and sisters; as change agents, let's be open to change. Let's sit down to exchange ideas and promote personal discovery and learning!

Outcome

The results of having a negative perception of change are defensiveness, manipulation, erosion of trust, political game playing, miscommunication, secrets, inflexibility, all-round ineffectiveness, and low commitment to congregational well-being.

Carey Garrett illustrates the communication that results from this negative perception through a case of accusations brought by a neighbor against Carey and her husband, Al. Carey and Al began building a carport on the side of their house. The neighbors had been accustomed to using Carey and Al's driveway to get to the alley. As construction proceeded, the neighbors raised the complaint that the new carport extended over the property line.

So Carey and Al met with the neighbors in what they describe as a high-tension meeting. Carey and Al felt sure the real reason for the upset was loss of access to the alley, not actually violation of boundaries. However, since the neighbor *stated* that their problem was with encroachment on the line, Carey and Al went along with the conversation, trying to resolve the boundary dispute. They spent some time haggling over surveyors' reports until, finally, the neighbor lady went back into her house for some documents. While she was gone, Al asked the man, "Why are you really upset?"

The neighbor then reluctantly admitted that the real issue was access to the alley. Carey and Al had played along, pretending the issue was the survey line, trying to avoid further conflict. However, their false conciliatory stance actually produced more tension overall. Carey observed that had she and Al gotten the real issue out in the open up front, they could have worked out solutions much sooner with less heat and probably would have created more openness and trust rather than defensiveness and tension.

On the other hand, the results of a positive perception of change are many. This stance generates *open* communication because the previously undiscussible things are put out on the table and dealt with. This perception produces *honest* communication, even though it sometimes means talking about the things that are hard to talk about. It also produces *flexibility* and *trust* and, it can result in genuine *commitment* to jointly generated changes. In short, an open-to-change mindset is by far the most productive for the would-be change agent.

Most people begin walking through the preceding graphic, subconsciously assuming they are learning how to determine the other guy's perception. Understanding the perceptions of others is important, of course; however, the greater value of this exercise is to help the change agent see his or her own perception of change and to evaluate his or her *own* conversational strategies or habits. This exercise even compels us to reexamine our own motives!

➤ Perceptions Determine How Values Are Expressed

To demonstrate the pervasive impact of our perceptions, let's look at how conversational strategies differ, even when the values of both styles are the same. The following chart assumes that those who are open to change and those who are closed to change both operate off of the same *Christian values.* However, the conversational strategies will vary greatly, because these strategies are largely determined by a person's perception of change, not by his or her values.

Christians of both styles want to care for, help, and support others. Both want to respect others; both value honesty; both want to embody strength and integrity.

Christian Values	Closed to Change	Open to Change
Care, Help, Support	Give approval and praise to others. Tell people what you think they want to hear.	Increase another's capacity to see their own perceptions.
Respect for Others	Defer to others; don't confront their reasoning or actions.	Encourage self-reflection and self-examination.
Honesty	Tell no lies or all you think and feel.	Say what is feared to say and encourage others to do so.
Strength	Advocate your position—win. Do not show weakness.	Advocate your position and inquire about others'.
Integrity	Stick to your principles, values, and beliefs.	Advocate your principles, values, and beliefs in a way that invites inquiry into them.

Figure 13. **The Expression of Christian Values**
Adapted from Chris Argyris[1]

Again, remember that we are not trying to "peg" people into fixed roles. However, as we examine how we and others communicate, we will improve our navigational skills.

Care, Help, Support

A closed-to-change person will show care, help, and support by giving approval and praise to others—telling them what he or she thinks they want to hear. I've made this mistake myself! The team with whom I work told me that my leadership style often tends toward the left-hand column. That is, I sometimes attempt to motivate people by verbalizing approval and praise, even when, in some cases, my body language screams the opposite! They say

I tend to ignore unpleasant reality and try to force pleasant reality into existence with flattering words.

In contrast, the open-to-change person will show care and support by increasing the other person's capacity to see their own perceptions. This open style respects and affirms the worth and capabilities of others. A more open approach in my personal working relationship would trust that my colleagues are responsible enough to handle the facts. This style demonstrates genuine care about the thoughts of my coworkers. An open style asks "why" questions: "Tell me more about your thinking on that." "Could you bring me up to speed on your rationale for doing it that way?" "What will you do if . . .?" "What will result when . . .?" "Have you considered . . .?" etc.

These two perceptions use totally different conversational strategies, although they operate off of the same values.

Respect for Others
Respect for others will be revealed very differently by those holding the two perceptions. The person who is closed to change defers to others by not confronting their reasoning or their actions. In contrast, the person who is open to change encourages self-reflection and self-examination. Across a decade of consulting with churches, I have observed that a number of church leaders tend to equate love, kindness, and gentleness with avoidance of the unpleasant; many simply will not surface problems. Thus, some churches are riddled with family secrets, which feed dysfunction.

Respectful openness, on the other hand, even though painful at times, produces much healthier systems in the long run. My staff colleague for years, Dr. Ed Coates, a marriage and family therapist, suggests that we respond to the secret scoop on knotty church problems by asking, "What happens when you talk about that?"

The response often sounds something like, "You've gotta be kidding! Talk about that!?" Discussion of loaded issues seems unthinkable to people with a negative perception of change. For them, to confront is to show disrespect. The truth is, however, that avoidance of openness and candidness may actually show lack of respect for a person's ability to deal responsibly with reality and to honestly self-examine. Avoidance can actually imply, "You are not capable of being a full player in a healthy system." It assumes that the other person is too dull to understand difficult reality or too delicate to handle it!

If we assume that a congregation does not want to face reality, we will likely attempt to cajole or manipulate adult people as if they were unable to deal with serious, painful, and complex issues. But again, healthy change is more likely when issues are out on the table. Argyris says that by the time an issue becomes "undiscussible," major resistance has already gathered.

Honesty

What conversational strategies are employed by the two different mindsets in their attempts to be honest? The person who perceives change as negative avoids lies, either by telling nothing (lest he ruffle some feathers) or by dumping out all his or her thoughts and feelings—regardless of the consequences. (Keith Miller calls this "The Vomit Theory of Honesty: puke up everything inside, no matter how bad it makes the environment stink.") In other words, the person who is closed to change either stuffs feelings or unloads them.

Wally Bullington is a dear friend and a longtime elder of my former church. For years he was a football coach, so his style of communication can be summed up as "the shortest distance between two points is a straight line." I love this trait in Wally because he never leaves you guessing about where he stands. One day years back, he walked into my office and, with few preliminaries, put his thoughts on the table, "I don't think you are doing your job." That was clear enough for even me to grasp!

So I said, "I don't really feel like I'm doing a very good job either. Which part of my job do you have reference to?"

Wally mentioned three or four specific things. My only honest response had to be, "True. You don't see me doing those things. But I did not understand those to be in my job description."

"I didn't know that," Wally responded. So we inventoried the things that needed doing that I wasn't doing. And after that conversation, Wally walked out and initiated a plan to add the staff person needed to cover what I had neither time nor talent to do. If Wally had assumed I could not handle that openness and had not been honest with me, we could have waltzed around the problem indefinitely—with my wondering what's going on, with Wally's disappointment in me growing, and with the task not getting done! This was an effective implementation of open conversational strategies on Wally's part. Of course, in addition to Wally's open style, he and I enjoyed a healthy personal relationship. We had gone fishing together. Carolyn and I had eaten at the Bullington's table many times. And I "chaplained" the college football team that Wally was coaching—so we had spent a lot of relational time together.

The open-to-change person says what is feared to say and encourages others to do so by making candidness safe. Even as I write these words, I am moved afresh with the complexity of change and with the importance of genuine relationships and healthy conversation to the process of navigating change. To say what one fears to say and to encourage others to do so is much safer with someone you eat, laugh, and pray with—someone whom you really trust and really love—than with people you view as strangers, opponents, or impediments to progress.

Good decisions about change won't happen without good information. Good information won't likely arise without plenty of authentic conversation. And authentic conversation happens best in real extended relationships.

Strength

The person who has a negative perception of change advocates his or her position in order to win. The closed-to-change person will express strength through such conversational strategies as: never show weakness, never let 'em see you sweat, and negotiate from a position of strength. While the person with a positive perception of change also advocates his or her position, this person uses conversational strategies that genuinely inquire into others' views and that invite dialogue between positions. Such strategies also invite examination of his or her own position so that flaws can be revealed and improvements made. This person looks for win-win solutions, not win-lose confrontations. The open style values synergism of combined ideas and believes that one plus one can equal far more than two.

Integrity

The last category is integrity. The closed-to-change person says "stick to your principles, values and beliefs— no matter what!" By contrast, the open-to-change person sticks to principles, values, and beliefs by advocating them in a way that allows inquiry into them. The open change-navigator freely puts his or her stuff up for examination and is willing to change in order to improve.

An observation: Historically, the dominant Church of Christ mindset has been "stick to your principles, values, and beliefs." We have stuck to principles tenaciously, but sometimes we did it in a closed way. Rather than advocating principles, values, and beliefs in a way that allows inquiry into them and invites others to do the same, our tendency has been to boast a column-two open philosophy but to practice a column-one closed. (See Figure 12.)

For example, in years past I have often "invited discussion" during my evangelistic messages, as did many of our preachers, by saying something like, "Please feel free to discuss these things with us. The truth has nothing to fear." We lauded the noble Bereans of Acts 17:11 who, unlike the closed-minded Thessalonians, were willing to search the Scripture to see if Paul's teaching was true. However, we often assumed that we had already searched the Scriptures and that others had not, so we didn't really plan on evaluating our own convictions when we ostensibly invited open inquiry. We did not expect to learn anything from others. Rather, we wanted to draw the "errors" of others into clear contrast with our "truth." In fact, those

among us who actually were willing to genuinely consider the validity of other views and learn something from
others—and to actually change our minds—were accused
of being soft and unstable on doctrine and not really stick-
ing to our guns.

We hope time is moving us as a people well over into
the open column. But quite often, church change-naviga-
tors stumble into hidden mine fields of explosive closed-
to-change people—not bad people, but people who
assume their views are the accurate view of reality, and
who thus genuinely feel that to seriously consider another
view equals dangerous compromise.

On the other end of the spectrum, those who have (or
at least fancy themselves to have) learned to perceive
change positively sometimes celebrate their newfound
enlightenment by attempting to force those with a negative perception of change to practice what conscience
does not free them to do. Ronnie Wiggins, director of the
Preston Road Center for Christian Education, says,
"Those who have freedom have multiple options. But
those who do not have freedom have only one option. So
it is unloving for the Christian with freedom to impose his
multiple options on the Christian who has only one option." This rings very true to me. I would only add that it
is also a very unloving thing to leave a fellow Christian
bound to only one option when genuine dialogue could
help that brother or sister find freedom.

We cannot overstress the importance of change agents
and church leaders personally examining their own perceptions and being constantly, personally open to change
themselves.

DIALOGUE VERSUS DISCUSSION

The two graphics in this chapter aid genuine dialogue and provide tools to help us better understand ourselves and others as we navigate the winds of change. Thusfar in this and the previous chapter, we have discussed four basic concepts:

1. Reality filtered (through beliefs, experiences, and assumptions) produces perceptions.

2. Perceptions affect strategy and structures—and thus outcomes.

3. Conversational strategies provide clues to perceptions of change.

4. Identifying perceptions of change facilitates change management.

With these concepts in hand, we are better prepared to move toward truly effective dialogue (conversation that allows us to come through to higher understanding) rather than participating in the percussion of mere discussion.

Effective dialogue combines compromise and synergism, and results in better changes brought about through healthier means. Such dialogue fosters positive proactive commitment rather that mere reluctant compliance. The open stance is threatening only if our real objective is flawed: to get my way, save my face, cover my tail, look effective, or the like. But if we really are driven by a desire to implement whatever enables the church to more effectively honor God and fulfill his mission—at whatever cost to ourselves—we have no fear of open dialogue. In this way, truth and trust tend to grow together. The apostle Paul beautifully describes the conversational style of a Christian:

If you have any encouragement from being united with Christ, if any comfort from his love, if any fellowship with the Spirit, if any tenderness and compassion, then make my joy complete by being like-minded, having the same love, being one in spirit and purpose. Do nothing out of selfish ambition or vain conceit, but in humility consider others better than yourselves. Each of you should look not only to your own interests, but also to the interests of others. (Phil. 2:1-4)

Efforts to change can prove dangerous without these basic principles concerning the nature, role, and power of our perceptions. The most significant transition happens at the level of perceptions, and perceptions are vastly improved through good conversation.

RESULTS OF CHANGE

"You know, what I discovered is that people from the outside think that the real differences are between conservatives and liberals. And the real difference as far as I can tell is people who believe in the future and people who are still living in the past."

President Bill Clinton[1]

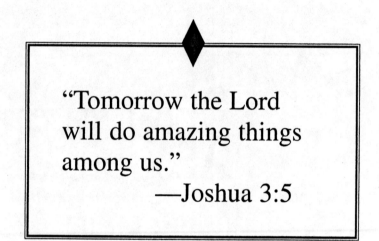

"Tomorrow the Lord
will do amazing things
among us."
———Joshua 3:5

CHAPTER FIFTEEN

*T*O DREAM AGAIN

For man is a dreamer ever . . .

I am more excited about the future of our fellowship these days than I have ever been in my life. I have more dreams now than ever. I feel more physically alive, more emotionally alive, more spiritually alive than ever I have in my life. If God would allow me the privilege to choose any lifetime slice of world history in which to live my life, I'd choose now, doing what I am doing, with our people. Why? Because, I feel that we are caught up in the stream of a new and mighty movement of God. He is unleashing something in our world that we have not seen in a long, long time. We see so many signs of hope!

No. These are not the Pollyanna ravings of an obscurantist dreamer. I am optimistic because of some specific, concrete, observable realities existing right now. Here are just a few:

GLOBAL ACTION

In 1974 Billy Graham and John Stott, alarmed at cutbacks in world missions, called a global congress of twenty-five hundred Christian leaders in Lausanne, Switzerland, to address the crisis. Fifteen years later, in 1989, they convened Lausanne II in Manila to assess progress. I was grateful to be one of the more than four thousand delegates who attended Lausanne II. One hundred and ninety nations were represented, the largest gathering of nations in history, including United Nations meetings.

On opening night, in the beautiful downtown Manila Convention Center, Tom Wang, heading the project, kicked things off with a video. The opening scene had been filmed three years prior on the Mount of Olives, where Wang handed torches to runners who set out to run "from Jerusalem, through Judea and Samaria, to the uttermost parts of the earth," to converge again at the congress in Manila. The video briefly tracked the runners through roadways of various nations, and then showed them running through the familiar streets of Manila.

As the video ended, the doors to the auditorium *swung* open, and down the aisles streamed the young runners— carrying flaming torches. Following them, in the colorful and varied costumes of national dress (and undress), came representatives of 190 nations. They converged on the stage, to deafening music and applause. Then Layton

Ford, Billy Graham's brother-in-law, shot the spotlight into the balcony, where seventy Russians, the first ever to be allowed to travel from the then Soviet Union for Christian purposes, stood and waved. The place went wild.

For eleven days we heard papers and reports, saw global video clips, prayed, worshiped, and met church leaders. Most exciting of all were the testimonies from the field. Progress between Lausanne I and Lausanne II had been astounding.

The global "Christian community" had more than doubled, nearly tripling in fifteen years.

The numerical locus of the Christian faith had shifted from North America to Southeast Asia, Latin America, and Africa. For example, in Seoul, Korea, three single congregations number more than one hundred thousand each.

A math teacher from Ghana who attended Lausanne I went back home and started a Bible study in his house. Now his Bible study group is a congregation of fifty thousand members, and they have started approximately one thousand daughter churches. We met another man who was sentenced to death and so fled his homeland, only to return repeatedly, undercover, to plant churches all over his country.

We heard from a woman from Addis Ababa who gave up enormous wealth and has endured several prison terms in order to care for the sick and starving in the slums.

We were deeply moved by a man from mainland China, probably only a little over fifty years of age, but so bent and broken that he looked seventy. He had spent seventeen years in prison. When he went into prison, he was leading an underground church of about five hundred. For the whole seventeen years, he could get no news about his church and feared it would scatter and disappear. But when he was released from prison, he found that his church had grown to fifteen thousand! Five of his years in prison had been spent in solitary confinement. For three years, he was forced daily to shovel human excrement in the cesspools. But when the guards distanced themselves because of the stench, he was free to voice the psalms and sing, "I come to the garden alone." He said, "God turned the cesspool into a garden of prayer." When he asked, "Would you rike me to sing it fo you"—and began, in his Chinese accent, to sing—"I come to da gadden arone, wye da dew is stiw on da roses"—If there was a dry eye in the audience of four thousand, I couldn't see it for the tears in mine.

Persecution, prison, and martyrdom are not just tales from ancient times. Paul and Silas were not the last preachers to be imprisoned or whipped for their faith. Almost every day, at some place in the world, Christians still put their lives on the line for my Lord and yours. Even this year several have been martyred.

Of course there was not unanimous theological agreement at Lausanne II. As someone said, "all Christian gatherings leave room for disagreement." But some words I heard repeatedly in Manila are familiar ones in our tradition. "Restoration" was a common theme. I heard proclamations that "the day of denominationalism is dead," and that "the Christian movement is free before Christ with a Bible in its hand." I tell you, something big is going on. I don't want to be caught throwing a Nerf ball on the back lot and miss the Super Bowl just on the other side of the wall.

Great things are happening globally in my own fellowship too! In 1990, my wife Carolyn and I visited three African countries. In Ethiopia—which suffered under communism, civil war, persecution and famine—the Church of Christ had grown from roughly fifteen to fifty thousand in fifteen years! In Kenya, Nigeria, and Zambia, the growth is amazing. Malawi has nearly one thousand congregations of Churches of Christ. I have recently returned from a visit to Brazil where solid growth flourishes. And just watch Eastern Europe! Celebrate—we are part of a cause that has no equal and that cannot fail! Strong winds are blowing!

NORTH AMERICAN ACTION

I stepped down from a platform after reporting the global excitement I'd seen in world missions, and this stuffy-looking "Brother Negative" collared me. "Okay. So things look good overseas, but nothing much is happening here at home. Churches cannot grow in North America."

Wrong!

Now, I did learn in Manila that the two most unreceptive fields in the world are the Muslim countries and North America (for very different reasons, of course). And it's also true that some third world Christian leaders are embarrassed by some brands of North American religion: the televangelist scandals, the show biz, the materialism, the offers of cheap grace. They know that not many people in the big churches of America would put their lives on the line for the gospel, as they themselves must

routinely do. They fear we are spoiled, and their perceptions are not all wrong.

Yet, in spite of all that, right here in North America,
many churches are booming and exploding at record
rates. Although few older churches are growing by evangelism, hundreds of younger churches are growing. The
Southern Baptists are the fastest growing denomination in
the country, but few of their old churches are reaching
unchurched people rapidly. Most of their phenomenal
growth is through new church plants. And look at the
free-church movement, Bible churches, and community
churches! Interestingly, some months after I left the
Highland Church of Christ pulpit, the rumor was circulated that Lynn Anderson had left the Church of Christ
and joined one of those nondenominational Bible
churches. I found this both amusing and revealing. To be
honest with you, all of my life I have been told I was already in one of those nondenominational Bible churches.
And I haven't left!

Of course, there are several different kinds of nondenominational Bible churches and community churches.
Hundreds of them are growing by reaching nonchurched
people. Besides, new churches spring up every week all
over the country. For example, one winter evening four
years ago, I picked up a car at Chicago's O'Hare Airport
and headed out through snow, wind, and twenty-one degree weather to visit a Wednesday evening church service. Five thousand people showed up (most of them
thirty minutes early) for ninety minutes of worship and
Bible teaching. I was impressed! So I hung around for
four days to see what was going on. I interviewed some
thirty-five people, staff and members. The more I learned,

the more impressed I became. On Sunday, over twelve thousand showed up—and that church was then only thirteen years old. The last time I visited that church, seven thousand came midweek with over fourteen thousand attending weekend services. But this is only one example from among nearly a thousand explosive growth stories in this country. In Los Angeles, one church, now thirteen years old, began in a living room and has grown to over seven thousand. It has started twenty-five daughter churches, none of which look exactly like the mother, and many of which are growing phenomenally.

My first reaction when I heard about these churches was, "This stuff must be a mile wide and an inch deep to market so well. Of course, if you cater to self-interest and if you dazzle people, you can gather a crowd. But if you ask people to stand up for Jesus and the Bible, 'like we do in the Restoration Movement,' that crowd would soon scatter."

But upon closer examination of a number of these churches, what has amazed me even more than the growth rate is the substance! I found myself thinking, "I have rarely been around this many believers in Christ who actually welcome higher demands on their own lives." Most of these churches claim the Bible as their only rule of faith and practice, require baptism, and are led by a plurality of scripturally qualified leaders. They call people to high levels of moral, financial, and ministry expectation. They consider that if you are not giving 10 percent, you are not living up to your commitment. If you are not plugged into a specific ministry, you are not considered a faithful member. Most expect accountability and practice firm church discipline. Far from being watered down, I found the expected commitment level in most growing churches to far exceed those in the average traditional Church of Christ.

Nothing in the message or demands in our congregations of the Church of Christ, or other traditional but slow-growing churches, would make them any less "marketable" than the message and demands I found in most of these rapidly growing mega-churches. In fact, many traditional church folks would scream bloody murder if called to similar standards. What then makes the difference? Why do some churches grow and other churches do not? Aside, of course, from the sovereignty of God and the obvious spiritual factors of church dynamics, the key difference is that these growing churches are connecting with the culture far more effectively than most traditional churches. They are thinking like the apostle Paul, when he said, "I have become all things to all men so that by all possible means I might save some" (1 Cor. 9:9). I am convinced that it is not our message, but our methods and our models and our mindset that "market" so poorly. Surely it is possible to "do church" biblically, yet in patterns that connect with our culture.

Fresh winds are blowing, and many, like the warm Chinook winds of the Northwest, are melting the chill which covers the earth!

A GROWING ARMY OF EFFECTIVE LEADERS

A third solid reason for my optimism about our future is the growing army of effective maturing younger men now leading many of our churches both as shepherds and as preachers. And hundreds more are coming up behind them.

SHEPHERDS NOT CEOS

In the last few years, as I have spent a great deal of time with church leaders, I have seen enormous changes among elders. Many who have watched from the pew for years are finally taking their leadership places and are saying, "The old ways of doing church are no longer working. We must do something different." Many seem willing to pay enormous prices for the changes needed to be effective in today's environment. No. I don't hear voices wanting to change the gospel or compromise the Bible. Quite to the contrary, a new generation of elders is searching for ways to change the methodology, change the design of our assemblies, change the way we communicate with the world, change the processes by which we grow people in the faith, even change their very style of leadership; but they are *not* seeking to change the Bible. In order to spread the gospel and teach the Bible more effectively, leaders in our fellowship are shifting back toward the cutting edge of the culture, where our forefathers were in 1865.

STRONG PULPITS

Working alongside the new breed of elders is a growing army of young ministers who are better trained than any previous generation of our preachers. They lift my hopes. Don't misunderstand me—I love our older preachers. In fact, I am one of them. But, our rapidly improving schools are turning out preachers who are light-years ahead of where I was at their age, with academic tools for Bible study far surpassing mine and those of most of my preaching peers. They love the Lord and the Bible, and they preach expository messages. They can crack the text in the original languages. In addition, they know how to communicate it to our world. And, in the spirit of the early restoration leaders, they know how to connect with the culture. Dozens are already at bat, with hundreds more on deck, and thousands in the dugout! Most of them read widely and many are trained in more than one field. Yes, some are frustrated out of their minds because they perceive the church as unwilling to implement the changes needed to connect with the culture. This makes the burden of this book all the more crucial. And many of the younger men show remarkable maturity and willingly face the rigorous task of becoming wise and skillful change agents.

Our younger ministers are also earning deep respect outside of our fellowship. An organization called Leadership Network hosts cross-denominational resource retreats for ministers. A number of our finest have participated in several of these conferences. Twice, I have heard executives of Leadership Network comment to the effect that, "after interfacing with all kinds of ministers, I perceive the guys from your fellowship to be among the brightest and the best." Every Sunday scores of thousands of people among Churches of Christ hear the preaching of these brightest and best ministers in most of our large, pacesetting churches. A bright new day is dawning.

The fresh winds are blowing more than hot air!

CHURCH PLANTINGS

Some older churches definitely are changing formats and strategies to be more effective, and some are showing signs of new growth, as church leaders learn how to navigate change without splitting churches. But I believe most of our growth in the next decade will come through new church plantings geared up to reach today's urban people. Scores of excellent young preachers will be teaming up with successful and godly business and professional people, pooling their resources for planting culturally appropriate new churches. New plants are under way in hundreds of cities, including many in our fellowship. Teams are forming for others. More and more students are thinking this way. In one graduate class I taught recently, well over half of the nineteen students aspired to be church planters. This new and exciting trend is evident among most religious and educational institutions.

We are dreaming again! My prayer is for that trend to flourish. I expect more new congregations to be planted across North America almost immediately—churches that will be rooted firmly in Scripture and that will connect with our times because they will be spiritually renewed, structurally reorganized, sociologically targeted, strategically intentional, streamlined and simplified, and zip-coded for the present age.

Planting churches is what it is all about, anyway. The ministry of apostle Paul focused on church plantings. He did not want to "build on another man's foundations."

For us, as for the Israelites who crossed over into a new world, "we have never been this way before," but "God will work wonders for us tomorrow" through the new army of effective church leaders. The winds of change may ruffle our feelings of security, but they are also scattering the seed of the kingdom. I am filled with anticipation and excitement these days. I dream. I get up in the mornings, charged with adrenaline.

We are part of a cause
that has no equal and
that cannot fail!

A GOD OF SURPRISES

Above all, my optimism is rooted in our God of surprises! "The Lord is my portion; therefore I will hope in him" (Lam. 3:24). In all of God's major movements, he has stunned the universe with surprise. No one could have anticipated what God would do next. Even the angels must have been caught of guard by the surprise of Creation. "Wow! Stars, planets, constellations, oceans and deserts, elephants and butterflies, rattlesnakes and roses—we never would have thought of that."

The exodus, too, was a mega-surprise. The people of God worked as slaves and walked like animals. With eyes on mud and straw—not on heaven—they could see no way out of Egypt. Then the God of surprises split the sea, led slaves out of bondage from mud to Mount Sinai, made them a nation, and put them back in touch with heaven. Who would have mapped this exit route or anticipated these mighty acts of God?

Surprise!

Again in the first century A.D.—when Israel had lost hope under the iron heel of Rome—came the mother of all surprises. God showed up in a manger, ended up on a cross, rose up from a grave, fired up a Pentecost—and shattered global darkness with a million points of light. How utterly unpredictable from a human standpoint.

The God of surprises stirred up the rushing of a mighty wind and blew history wide open . . . again at the enlightenment . . . and through the industrial revolution . . . and at the Reformation . . . and in the Restoration Movement.

Only Rip Van Winkle could miss the most recent surprises of God. If, five years ago, I had predicted that the Berlin wall would fall within two years, you would have questioned my sanity. But, in one globe-shaking week, God scattered the Berlin wall to knickknack shelves around the world. He dismantled not only the wall, but the whole Soviet Union and world Communism!

What if I had tried in 1988 to convince you that, by 1991, our brothers and sisters would be preaching the gospel over Russian national TV at government expense and teaching the Bible in Russian public schools? You would have dismissed me out of hand. But the God of surprises has had us doing these things for two years now!

God is full of surprises and capable of anything! Why, even Nelson Mandela, once rotting in a South African prison, is coauthor of South African Racial Civil Rights and corecipient of the Nobel Peace prize, along with none other than F. W. deKlerk! What next? Surely the God of

surprises can and will awaken the church, shift our strategies, connect us with the nerve centers of our culture, and
shake the planet yet again.

Some years back, a family from London, England,
camping in the Scottish Highlands, pitched their tent near
the foot of a towering waterfall that spilled from the crags
above and roared through a gorge below. The spot was
wilderness, except for a family of Scottish shepherds
camped further downstream. In a careless moment the
preteen son of the Londoners fell into the raging current
and was swept down the gorge. The boy would certainly
have perished in the rocks and foam but for the youthful
son of the shepherds who, without thought for his own
safety, leaped into the torrent to rescue the young
Londoner. In a few moments, both families gathered
around the two wet and frightened little boys who were
still blinking water from their eyes.

The Londoners, overwhelmed with gratitude, offered
money to the shepherd lad. But the shepherds refused it,
"We can't allow him to take money for such a thing as
that." So the grateful parents asked the shepherd family,
"Where does your boy go to school?"

The somewhat awkward reply came, "In this part of
Scotland, the children of shepherds rarely go to school."

"Then that's it," exclaimed the Londoners, "Why not
let your son come with us to London and go to school
with our son?"

The unlettered shepherd boy went to London and to
school. Although he started slowly, soon he did quite well
in his studies. He went on to university, graduating with
high honors; then to medical school, gaining national ac-
claim as a brilliant research physician. His name was

Alexander Fleming: he lives in history as the man who discovered penicillin.

Oh, yes, and the little fellow he fished out of the stream? His name was Winston—Winston Churchill—who was to become prime minister of Great Britain.

Had we stood by that Scottish highland stream that day, searching the upturned faces of those two little boys, we would never have dreamed what it meant to be looking into the eyes of Alexander Fleming and Winston Churchill. But God knew! And God is a God of surprises. Who knows what the God of surprises will do around our next corner. When I look into the face of a child I often wonder, "Could this be the next Fleming or Churchill . . . or Moses or Paul or Luther or Campbell or Billy Graham or Mother Teresa?"

Maybe it is that person sitting in the class you teach or playing on your little league team, or one who lives at your house and eats at your table. Maybe it could even be you! To paraphrase Joshua, "Consecrate yourselves and tomorrow the God of surprises may blow your doors off!"

The God of surprises is a God of hope. So, for as long as I allow myself to be called his servant, I will traffic in hope! These are not times to give up. We must be risk takers. We must track what the Spirit is doing on the cutting edges of the kingdom. In the tradition of the men of Issachar, we will attempt to "understand the times" so that we will "know what to do" (1 Chron. 12:31). We are part of a cause that has no equal and that cannot fail!

> Man is a dreamer ever,
>   He glimpses the hills afar
> And dreams of the things out yonder . . .

. . . when the God of surprises stirs up the winds of the Spirit and blows our doors off!

RESOURCES ON CHANGE MANAGEMENT

Allen, Jere and George Bullard. *Shaping a Future for the Church in the Changing Community.* Atlanta: Home Mission Board, 1981.

Anderson, Leith. *The Church at the End of the Twentieth Century.* Minneapolis: Bethany House Publishers, 1991.

_____. *Dying for Change.* Minneapolis: Bethany House Publishers, 1990.

Anderson, Lynn. Hope Network. 12801 N. Central Expy., Ste. 1560, Dallas, TX 75243. (800) 238-0866.

Argyris, Chris. *Overcoming Organizational Defenses.* Needham Heights, MA: Allyn & Bacon, 1990.

Barker, Joel Arthur. *Future Edge.* New York: William Morrow and Co., 1992.

Barna, George. *Marketing the Church.* Colorado Springs, CO: NavPress, 1991.

_____. *User Friendly Church.* Ventura, CA: Regal Books, 1991.

_____. *Turnaround Churches.* Ventura, CA: Regal Books, 1993.

Beam, Joe. Change Dynamics International. 171 Kestwick Dr. E, Martinez, GA. 30907. (706) 855-9900.

Bridges, William. *Managing Transitions.* Reading, MA.: Addison-Wesley Publishing Co., 1991.

_____. *Transitions: Making Sense of Life's Changes.* Reading, MA: Addison-Wesley Publishing Co., 1980.

Church That Connects, A., I and *II.* Hope Network, 12801 N. Central Expy. Ste. 1560, Dallas, TX 75243. (800) 238-0866. (Cassettes and notebook.)

Connor, Daryl R. *Managing at the Speed of Change.* New York: Random House, 1993.

Davis, Stanley M. *Future Perfect.* Reading, MA: Addison-Wesley Publishing Co., 1987.

Drucker, Peter. *The New Realities.* New York: Harper & Row, Publishers, 1988.

Garrett, Carey. 3321 Lovers Lane, Dallas, TX 75225. (214) 692-5739.

George, Carl. "How to Handle Conflict and Change," Audio Seminar Series, 1991. Fuller Institute. P.O. Box 91990, Pasadena, CA 91109-1990. (800) 999-9578. (Cassettes and study notes.)

Roozen, David A. and C. Kirk Hadaway. *Church and Denominational Growth.* Nashville: Abingdon Press, 1993.

Schaller, Lyle E. *Strategies for Change.* Nashville: Abindgon Press, 1993.

Senge, Peter M. *The Fifth Discipline.* New York: Doubleday, 1990.

RESOURCES ON WORSHIP

Allen, Robert and Gordon Borror. Worship: *Rediscovering the Missing Jewel.* Portland, OR: Multnomah, 1982.

Dozier, Dan. Unpublished manuscript on worship. Madison Church of Christ, 106 Gallatin Road, Madison, TN 37115. (615) 860-3206.

Hayford, Jack. et. al. *Mastering Worship.* Portland, OR: Multnomah, 1990.

Leaven. Winter Quarter 1990. c/o Mark Love, 24375 S.E. Stark, Gresham OR 97030. (503) 666-8485.

Olbricht, Thomas. "Back to the Future: Thoughts on Transmitting Our Heritage in Worship to the Next Generation." Christian Scholars' Convention 1993

Papers. Harding University, Box 2280, Searcy, AR 72149.

Peterson, Eugene. *Answering God.* New York: Harper & Row, 1989.

Reese, Jack. "Some Thoughts on the General State of Congregational Worship Among American Churches of Christ." Christian Scholars' Convention 1993 Papers. Harding University, Box 2280, Searcy, AR 72149.

Shelly, Rubel. Dinner Speech. *A Church That Connects II.* August 14, 1993. Hope Network, 12801 N. Central Expressway, Suite 1560, Dallas, TX 75243.

Taylor, Jack R. *Hallelujah Factor.* Nashville: Broadman Press, 1983.

Webber, Robert E. *Worship Is a Verb.* Dallas: Word, 1985.

_____. *Worship: Old and New.* Grand Rapids, MI: Zondervan, 1982.

"What's Drama Doing in Church?" *Leadership.* Summer 1993, pp. 51-58.

Willomon, William H. *With Glad and Generous Heart.* Nashville: The Upper Room, 1987.

APPENDIX C

RESOURCES ON THE CHURCH

Allen, Leonard. *The Cruciform Church.* Abilene, TX: Abilene Christian University Press, 1990.

Dulles, Avery. *Models of the Church.* Garden City, NY: Image Books, 1978.

Shelly, Rubel and Randall J. Harris. *The Second Incarnation.* West Monroe, LA: Howard Publishing, 1992.

Woodroof, James S. *The Church in Transition.* Searcy, AR: The Bible House, Inc., 1990.

APPENDIX D

RESOURCES ON MUSIC

Seay, Albert. *Music in the Medieval World.* Englewood Cliff, NJ: Prentice-Hall, 1975.

Squire, Russel N. *Church Music.* St. Louis: Bethany, 1962.

2. George Barna, Marketing the Church (Colorado Springs: NavPress, 1991), 21.

Chapter four. YOU *CAN* TEACH AN OLD DOG NEW TRICKS

1. Lynn Anderson, *An Interview,* Part One, *Image Magazine,* Vol. VII, #3, May-June 1991, 15.
2. Stanley M. Davis, *Future Perfect* (Reading, MA: Addison-Wesley Publishing Co., 1987), 8.
3. Peter F. Drucker, *The New Realities* (New York: Harper & Row Publishers, 1989).
4. Leith Anderson, *Dying for Change* (Minneapolis: Bethany House Publishers, 1990).

Chapter five. FORM FOLLOWS FUNCTION: THEOLOGICAL FOUNDATIONS

1. Ray S. Anderso*n, Theological Foundation for Ministry* (Grand Rapids: T. and T. Clark, Ltd., 1979), 8.

Chapter six. LIFE SPANS: RESPECTING THE PAST

1. Robert D. Dale, *Keeping the Dream Alive* (Nashville: Broadman Press, 1988) and *To Dream Again,* (Nashville: Broadman Press, 1981).

Chapter seven. A CHURCH THAT CONNECTS

1. Rubel Shelly, *A Church That Connects II* Dinner Speech, August 14, 1993. Order transcript from Hope Network, 12801 N. Central Expy., Ste. 1560, Dallas, TX 75243.

2. *Dallas Morning News* "Mighty Fortresses: Mega-Churches Try to Be All Things to Busy People" from *The Wall Street Journal* May 13, 1991, A6.

3. George Barna, Application Guide to *User Friendly Church:* The Audio Companion to the Best Selling Book (Barna Research Group, Ltd. Glendale, CA, 1991), 7.

4. Lyle Schaller, *Growing Plans* (Nashville: Abingdon Press, 1983), 115.

Chapter eight. RIGHT-BRAINED CHRISTIANS IN A LEFT BRAINED CHURCH

1. George Barna, "The Church Growth Without Compromise" seminar, Dallas, May 14-16, 1992.

2. "Sweet, Sweet Spirit," Dori Akers, (Manna Music, Inc., 1962).

Chapter nine. MUSIC THAT MAKES SENSE

1. Russel N. Squire, *Church Music* (St. Louis: Bethany Press, 1962).

Chapter ten. MINIMIZING CHAOS

1. Peter Senge, *The Fifth Discipline* (New York: Doubleday, 1990), 57-60.

2. "To a Mouse," Burns' *Poems and Songs* (London: Oxford University Press, 1969), 69.

3. Story idea comes from Theodore H. White, *The Making of the President* (MacMillan Press, 1989).

4. Fred Craddock, "The Shock of Recognition," tape 93 from *Preaching Today,* monthly sermons produced by *Christianity Today* and *Leadership,* 465 Gunderson Dr., Carol Stream, IL 60188.

5. Lyle Schaller, *Strategies for Change* (Nashville: Abingdon Press, 1993), 10-11.

6. William Bridges, *Managing Transition* (Reading, MA: Addison-Wessley Publishing Co., 1991).

7. Everett M. Rogers, *Communication of Innovations* (New York: Collier-MacMillan Publisher, 1971), 182.

Chapter eleven. GETTING CHANGE INTO YOUR SYSTEM

1. Edwin Friedmann, *Generation to Generation* (New York: Puilford Press, 1985).

2. Peter Senge, *The Fifth Discipline* (New York: Doubleday, 1990), 57-66.

3. Daryl Connor, *Managing at the Speed of Change* (New York: Random House, 1993), 104.

4. *Alcoholics Anonyous,* 3rd edition (New York: Alcoholics Anonymous World Services, Mc., 1976).

Chapter twelve. TRANSITION OR JUST CHANGE?

1. William Bridges, *Managing Transition* (Reading, MA: Addison: Wesley Publishing Co., 1991), 70.

2. P. Maris, *Loss and Change* (New York: Anchor Press/Doubleday, 1975), 66.

Chapter thirteen. CHANGING PERCEPTIONS

1. Chris Argyris, *Overcoming Organizational Defenses* (Needham Heights, MA: Allyn & Bacon, 1990), 88.

2. Ibid.

Chapter fourteen. CONVERSATION: WINDOWS INTO PERCEPTIONS

1. Chris Argyris, *Overcoming Organizational Defenses* (Needham Heights, MA: Allyn & Bacon, 1990), 19-21.

Chapter fifteen. TO DREAM AGAIN

1. Bill Clinton, *Dallas Morning News,* Nov. 28, 1993.

NAVIGATING the *Winds* of CHANGE

HOW CAN YOUR CHURCH MANAGE CULTURAL CHANGE WITHOUT COMPROMISING ETERNAL TRUTHS?

Many churches are currently grappling with this question, and this important book by Lynn Anderson is full of answers.

The winds of change are blowing, and they will not be ignored. Churches that learn how to successfully manage the changes these winds bring will sail smoothly into the 21st century. Congregations that close their eyes to the reality of change will be swept off course or into extinction.

In this book, Anderson—a well-known author, minister, and leader—presents a wealth of practical, effective strategies for managing change in the church. He is the creative force behind the annual "Church That Connects" seminar that has helped hundreds of church leaders manage positive change in their congregations; and now he gives these vital strategies directly to you.

"This book is filled with heart-warming stories, fresh insights, and proven strategies for relevant, Bible-based change in our congregations. Thanks, Lynn, for a message filled with optimism, joy, and hope."

> Dr. Kregg Hood, Minister
> South MacArthur Church of Christ

"Finally, here is a book about managing change in the church that gives realistic encouragement, authentic hope, and practical solutions. A powerhouse book that I couldn't put down."

> Dr. Jerry Rushford
> Pepperdine University

An increasing number of churches in our country are experiencing tension over worship styles, leadership roles, and direction. While the problem is often viewed as generational and contextual, it is also spiritual. If God is really leading us, we will be changing constantly in our efforts to be transformed into his glory. Anderson's positive contribution helps point change in a _____

ISBN 1-878990-31-4

90000

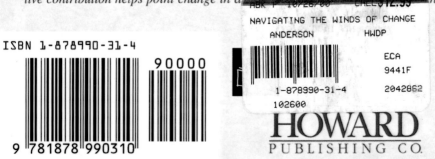

ABK 1 10/26/00   CHEC $12.99
NAVIGATING THE WINDS OF CHANGE
ANDERSON   HWDP
                  ECA
                  9441F
1-878990-31-4   2042862
102600

9 781878 990310

HOWARD
PUBLISHING CO.

NOTES

Prologue. FACING THE CHILL WINDS OF CHANGE

1. Larry McMurty, *Streets of Laredo* (New York: Simon and Schuster, 1993), 13, 18, 21, 22.

2. Leith Anderson, *Dying for Change* (Minneapolis: Bethany House Publishers, 1990), 11.

3. George Barna, "Understanding Ministry in a Changing Culture." Seminar. Barna Research Group, 647 W. Broadway, Glendale, CA 91204-1007

4. Carey Garrett, Change Management Consultant for EDS Management Consulting Services, Plano, TX.

5. Randy Lowry and Richard Myers, *Conflict Management and Counseling* (Dallas: Word, 1991).

6. William Bridges, *Managing Transition* (Reading, MA: Addison-Wesley Publishing Co., 1991). Peter M. Senge, *The Fifth Discipline* (New York: Doubleday, 1990). Chris Argyris, *Overcoming Organizational Defenses* (Needham Heights, MA: Allyn & Bacon, 1990). Daryl R. Connor, *Managing at the Speed of Change* (New York: Random House, 1993).

Chapter one. SHATTERED DREAMS

1. "Deore's World," *The Dallas Morning News*, Nov. 22, 1993.
2. Tony Buzan, *Use Both Sides of Your Brain* (New York: Penguin, 1989), 18-19.
3. J. Wallace Hamilton, *Horns and Halos in Human Nature* (Old Tappan, NJ: Fleming H. Revell Co., 1950), 120.
4. Mac Lynn, *Churches of Christ in the United States* (Nashville: Gospel Advocate Co., 1992), xviii.
5. George Barna, *The Frog in the Kettle* (Ventura, CA: Regal Books, 1985).
6. David A. Roozen and C. Kirk Hadaway, *Church and Denominational Growth,* Abingdon Press, Nashville, 1993.
7. William Willomon, *Clergy and Laity Burnout* (Nashville: Abingdon Press, 1987), 25-26.
8. William Herbert Carruth, "Dreamers of Dreams," *Masterpieces of Religious Verse* (New York: Harper & Brothers, 1948), 278.

Chapter two. WHAT WENT WRONG?

1. Lyle Schaller, conversation with author, 1990.
2. Frank Tillapaugh, *Unleashing the Church* (Ventura, CA: Regal Books, 1985).

Chapter three. WHY CHANGE?

1. . William Bridges, "Handling Transition Successfully," 1993 Church in the 21st Century Conference, Orlando, FL. (800) 776-5454 (Convention Cassaettes).